T0004943

"*Thriving Families* offers a unique perspective on how we can care for children who come from hard places. This book values and amplifies voices in a way that makes the reader truly want to listen and learn alongside their community for the sake of God's children."

TORI HOPE PETERSEN, bestselling author of *Fostered*

"Foster care and adoption is an imperfect solution to an impossible problem on this side of heaven. However, that doesn't mean we sit on our hands until God's kingdom comes. And thanks to people like Jenn and Josh Hook, their work, and awesome resources like this book, we are able to have our hands steadied and strengthened for the work ahead. *Thriving Families* is a tangible and digestible tool that covers all important and necessary areas for the family and the individual. It doesn't matter whether you are considering a yes, recently said yes, or said yes decades ago, this book is for you."

GAELIN ELMORE, former foster youth, child welfare advocate, and speaker

"Drawing on their combined clinical expertise and real-world experiences working with foster and adoptive families, Jenn Hook and Joshua Hook offer page after page of wisdom that will empower and encourage parents, caregivers, and other caring adults."

JOSH SHIPP, author of the children's book *No Matter What: A Foster Care Tale*

"The Hooks do it again! They bring us the gospel truth while connecting deeply with our hearts. As you read through the pages of this book, you will find yourself compelled by the stories they share, challenged in your assumptions, and encouraged as you gain practical tools to take your next step. I believe *Thriving Families* has the potential to make a transformational impact on your parenting and family!"

JAMI KAEB, founder and executive director of The Forgotten Initiative

"*Thriving Families* is a beautiful resource for families who are on the complex path to adoption or foster care. The Hooks not only provide a toolkit to help set families up for success, but also give a voice to families who often go unheard. This book gives hope to families who may feel alone on this extraordinary journey."

NICOLE ARGO, former foster youth, now mother of two and a pastor's wife

"A great resource full of wisdom and expertise! It will be one that parents refer back to because it provides knowledge and practical strategies for adoptive families, foster families, and those seeking to support them. It is written with care, love, and a deep desire to make a difference in the life of every child and family that is standing in the gap for them. The Hooks knocked it out of the park!"

JT OLSON, founder of the Both Hands Foundation

"I am a foster care alumnus and someone who has seen firsthand the incredible work done through Jenn and Josh Hook's Replanted ministry. This book does a phenomenal job of illustrating through lived experiences the sometimes rocky and sharp elements of this beautiful foster and adoptive family mosaic. Loving and raising kids who didn't come from your body isn't for wimps, but with high risk comes high reward—for us, for our communities, and for the kingdom of God. Thanks to the Hooks for this work, may we never be the same."

LISA F. BARNES, former foster youth, Salvation Army officer, author, and international speaker

THRIVING FAMILIES

THRIVING
FAMILIES

a **TRAUMA-INFORMED GUIDEBOOK**
for the **FOSTER** *and* **ADOPTIVE JOURNEY**

JENN RANTER HOOK
founder of Replanted Ministry
JOSHUA N. HOOK, PHD

HERALD
P R E S S

Harrisonburg, Virginia

Herald Press
PO Box 866, Harrisonburg, Virginia 22803
www.HeraldPress.com

Library of Congress Cataloging-in-Publication Data
Names: Hook, Jenn Ranter, author. | Hook, Joshua N., author.
Title: Thriving families : a trauma-informed guidebook for the adoptive and
   foster journey / Jenn Ranter Hook, Joshua N. Hook.
Description: Harrisonburg, Virginia : Herald Press, [2023] | Includes
   bibliographical references.
Identifiers: LCCN 2022034380 (print) | LCCN 2022034381 (ebook) | ISBN
   9781513810478 (paperback) | ISBN 9781513810485 (hardcover) | ISBN
   9781513810492 (ebook)
Subjects: LCSH: Parent and child--Religious aspects--Christianity. |
   Families--Religious aspects--Christianity. | Adoptive parents | Foster
   parents. | Adopted children--Psychology. | Foster children--Psychology.
Classification: LCC BV4529 .H634 2023 (print) | LCC BV4529 (ebook) | DDC
   248.8/45--dc23/eng/20221003
LC record available at https://lccn.loc.gov/2022034380
LC ebook record available at https://lccn.loc.gov/2022034381

Study guides are available for many Herald Press titles at www.HeraldPress.com.

THRIVING FAMILIES
© 2023 by Jenn Ranter Hook and Joshua N. Hook
Released by Herald Press, Harrisonburg, Virginia 22803. 800-245-7894. All rights reserved.
Library of Congress Control Number: 2022034380
International Standard Book Number: 978-1-5138-1047-8 (paperback);
      978-1-5138-1048-5 (hardcover); 978-1-5138-1049-2 (ebook)
Printed in United States of America

All rights reserved. This publication may not be reproduced, stored in a retrieval system, or transmitted in whole or in part, in any form, by any means, electronic, mechanical, photo-copying, recording or otherwise without prior permission of the copyright owners.

All scripture quotations, unless otherwise indicated, are taken from the Holy Bible, New International Version®, NIV®. Copyright © 1973, 1978, 1984, 2011 by Biblica, Inc.® Used by permission of Zondervan. All rights reserved worldwide. www.zondervan.com The "NIV" and "New International Version" are trademarks registered in the United States Patent and Trademark Office by Biblica, Inc.®

27 26 25 24 23   10 9 8 7 6 5 4 3 2 1

*To the children who shared their sacred
thoughts, feelings, and experiences with me.
Your voice matters.*

—JENN RANTER HOOK

*To my daughter Autumn,
who made me a father for the first time.*

—JOSHUA N. HOOK

CONTENTS

FOREWORD

We were waiting in baggage claim after the long flight from Ethiopia. My husband was exhausted. Our new daughter, on the other hand, ran through the airport as we tried to contain her. Her tiny frame was filled with frenetic energy. Russ and I smiled bravely, but we were flooded with uncertainty. How were we going to get her out of the airport and into the car without creating a scene?

We became adoptive parents with a degree of confidence. After all, we were already parenting seven kids and doing a pretty good job. We loved the life we'd created. Adopting children from an Ethiopian orphanage seemed to be a beautiful meeting of the desire of our hearts to love our children and follow our passion for serving God.

I had been excited and energized as we prepared. In addition to my obsessive reading of blogs by adoptive moms, we read books and went to a weekend training with our agency. Then we traveled to Ethiopia, and there my confidence wavered.

We quickly realized one of our four new children had needs beyond the scope of the books we'd read. In the darkness of the Addis Ababa nights, my husband and I whispered our fears to each other. Surely she would settle in once we were home. We believed we would give our new children so much love and gentle care that, in time, they would be absorbed into our family and all would be well.

Sixteen years have passed since that day in the airport. We began our journey as adoptive parents attempting to fit our new children into the parenting style, educational methods, and life we'd carefully cultivated. We had a lot to learn.

We were humbled by our loving God, who gently led us to a new way of parenting our children. We turned our focus to connection over correction, looking for the needs behind the behaviors, and putting the relationship at the center of every interaction.

During those years, I had the privilege of meeting Jenn and Joshua Hook. Jenn is the founder and executive director of Replanted and the creator of its corresponding conference, at which I've been honored to speak several times. Jenn's wide smile and warm personality made me wish for a long conversation over coffee. Let's be honest, who of us wouldn't grab the opportunity to sit with a trauma-informed therapist, especially one devoted to foster and adoptive families? If you're like me, you'd come with a list of questions tucked in your pocket.

Fortunately, reading *Thriving Families* is like sitting down with two wise friends who understand families like ours. As Jenn writes, "I wanted to give every adoptive and foster parent a toolkit of helpful interventions and strategies they can use *today* to help parent their child." And that's just what she and Joshua have done with this book.

Thriving Families is a comprehensive resource for foster and adoptive parents. Jenn and Joshua have created a clearly organized path for you to follow. They begin by establishing a solid foundation for foster care and adoption, then provide you with a robust knowledge base, and finally give you a weighty toolbox packed with practical tools and helpful interventions.

The authors don't shy away from hard topics. I'm particularly thankful for the chapters on cultural and social adjustment and grief and loss, which are often neglected in books for foster and adoptive families. As a mom of transracially adopted teens and a former foster mom, I urge you to pay particular attention to them.

Whether you are preparing to foster or adopt or your children have been home for years, this expert guide will be one of your best resources. *Thriving Families* will meet needs you didn't even know you had. You'll find yourself pulling it off the shelf time and time again.

Press on in the good work to which you've been called. God is faithfully walking every step with you.

—Lisa Qualls
Coauthor (with Dr. Karyn Purvis) of *The Connected Parent: Real-Life Strategies for Building Trust and Attachment* and cofounder of The Adoption Connection

PREFACE

Ever since I (Jenn) can remember, I've had a huge heart for kids. When I was growing up and first learning about different jobs, I thought it would be cool to be a neonatal intensive care nurse. I ended up going a different route and got my master's degree in clinical psychology, but I always knew I wanted to work with kids. And after I graduated, one of my first jobs was at a foster care agency, counseling kids and their families.

This was difficult work, and it opened my eyes to the complexity of what children affected by adoption and foster care experience. Before I had the privilege of sitting with these children and hearing their stories, I believed the popular narrative among Christians that (1) children in foster care and orphanages needed us, (2) their birth families were often terrible, (3) our homes were better options for these children, and (4) love was enough to heal all wounds. Maybe you have believed this narrative yourself.

Over time, my experiences challenged many of these beliefs. For example, I learned that many children who grew up in orphanages actually had some family connections—but for some reason their biological family felt that they were unable to care for them. Many of the children I worked with had experienced really hard things, and all were there because something traumatic had separated them from their birth parents, either temporarily or permanently. However, I also had a chance to work with many of the foster families caring for these children, as well as the birth families trying to reunify with their children. Many of the birth parents had grown up in difficult situations themselves. Many of the foster parents were struggling. Children continued to have a tough time despite the change in environment. I facilitated final visits between children in foster care and their birth families—many children cried and held their parents tight because they didn't want to say goodbye. These situations were complex, and there were no easy answers. As I sat with these children and families—developing quite a bit of understanding and empathy for everyone involved—I began to realize the narrative needed to shift if we are going to support our children in the best way possible.

In my work as a counselor with the foster care agency and then later as the founder of a nonprofit organization called Replanted, which helps support adoptive and foster families, I've met and heard the stories of hundreds of adoptive and foster families who are doing their best to navigate this complexity and love the children in their care well. When I ask families how they are doing, the response is usually mixed. Many families feel a unique call to care for their children and families, with a clear sense from God that this is what they should be doing with their lives. But parenting children through adoption and foster care can be difficult and challenging. If you are reading this book, you have almost certainly experienced that. Many of our kids are facing a tough road, and sometimes it can be easy to lose faith when the challenges keep mounting.

Through my work as a counselor and as the leader of Replanted, it became clear to me that some important tools and strategies can be helpful for parenting children through adoption and foster care, but few parents had a good understanding and grasp of these tools and strategies. This wasn't the parents' fault. Training and education for adoption and foster parents got mixed reviews—some parents felt prepared for their journey, and others did not. I kept thinking it would be great if parents didn't have to see a trauma-informed therapist in order to learn some of these tools and strategies (although I love therapy and recommend it to everyone). That's why I wrote this book—I wanted to give every adoptive and foster parent a toolkit of helpful interventions and strategies they can use *today* to help parent their child.

Don't get me wrong—parenting through the complexities of adoption and foster care can and will be hard. When kids have experienced significant trauma, there are no easy fixes. And using these strategies doesn't guarantee that you will always get the outcome you want. But they will help you understand the unique realities that children affected by adoption and foster care experience and will position you to help your child recognize and realize their potential—and help you love and support your child right where they are. Parenting through adoption and foster care is holy work, work that is so close to the heart of God. There is something beautiful about the commitment to walk alongside a child who has experienced trauma and consistently demonstrate God's infinite, unconditional love. I'm glad we're on this journey together!

Part I

INTRODUCTION AND FOUNDATION

FLIP THE SCRIPT

At our annual Replanted Conference, where adoptive and foster parents and caregivers gather to be equipped, inspired, and refreshed, we offer a type of talk called "Flip the Script." Attendees often tell us that these are some of their favorite talks of the entire conference. These talks offer a fresh and unexpected perspective from someone whose voice isn't often given a platform but whose experience has something important for all of us to hear.

When you attend a conference, most of the time you listen to an expert or educator explain something new or tell you how to do something difficult. And this is a good thing—we need experts! But this type of talk is . . . well, expected. You know there will probably be a PowerPoint presentation and three main points—maybe all starting with the same letter so you can remember them better.

The Flip the Script talks are different. These talks amplify the voices of adopted persons, foster alumni, and birth parents—voices that aren't often heard in these conversations. Instead of inviting an expert to teach, we invite people with lived experience to share their perspective.

It's important to listen to and honor the experiences of those most directly involved in and affected by the journey of adoption and foster care. A "top down" approach, where experts drive the conversation, can sometimes miss the mark. We may not have a good sense of what our children are actually struggling with, or what they truly need. Guidance from experts can be helpful in our children's healing process, but to best care for children through adoption and foster care, we also need to hear from those with lived experience. We need both sets of voices. Their unique perspective offers an inside scoop so we can best care for our kids, their experiences, and the internal dialogue or questions they may be wrestling with.

That is what we have tried to do in this book—flip the script by using our experiences with adoptive and foster families to gather the best information about what has worked in their parenting. Throughout each of our journeys, we have talked with hundreds of adoptive and foster families and listened to their experiences. We have heard about many things that were going well—unique strengths of adoptive and foster families. And we have heard about things that were not going as well—difficulties, hardships, and challenges.

Let's be honest: parenting can be a struggle. It's the one job you don't get any training for! After I became a mom and started to raise my daughter, everything was a new learning experience for me. Some of these learning experiences were fun, and some were really, really hard. And as my daughter has grown and changed over the years, the learning, the fun, and the hard parts continue.

Parenting a child through adoption or foster care has additional challenges. Your child may have experienced trauma, and even if it happened long ago, they may still experience its lingering effects. Your child might have trouble attaching to you—and even though you try so hard to connect with them, nothing seems to work. Or maybe your child processes information from the world differently, and it's hard to keep them focused and comfortable. Perhaps your child is wrestling with what life would have been like if they were able to stay with their birth family, and it brings up something painful inside you.

Unique cultural factors are at play when you are an adoptive or foster family. You might be in a transracial family and want to support your child's cultural identity, but you don't know how. Even if your child shares your race or ethnicity, they are coming from a different family system, and there is often a period of adjustment as you try to merge your differing perspectives, expectations, and assumptions. Or maybe your child has mixed feelings about the placement—and you aren't sure what to do with that.

Our goal in this book is twofold: First, we aim to provide a balanced perspective about some of the issues and challenges that adoptive and foster families face, particularly in regard to parenting their children. Parenting is tough! We don't want to avoid the difficult conversations; instead, we want to talk about them openly, offering grace every step of the way.

Second, we want to share tools and strategies for helping kids heal, grow, and thrive. These strategies are applicable to parenting all kids, but they are particularly useful for adoptive and foster families. If you are a parent who needs some help (couldn't we all!), you're in the right place.

WHO THIS BOOK IS FOR

At its core, this book is for parents raising kids through adoption and foster care (including kinship care). As noted, the issues we talk about in the book likely apply in some way to all parenting scenarios, but there are some specific ways they are helpful for adoptive and foster families to consider. If you are an adoptive or foster parent and you're struggling with your parenting journey, you are not alone—this book is for you. Even if you aren't currently struggling, we believe this book will be helpful for you. It's important to be prepared for the various ways that adoption and foster care shapes your child's journey through all their developmental stages.

We also had two other groups of people in mind when we wrote this book. First, this book is for those who are thinking about adopting or fostering. So many people start their adoption or foster care parenting journey not really knowing what they are getting themselves into and experience a jarring wake-up call when the reality of their situation doesn't match their expectations. The more prepared you can be, the better. So if you are considering adopting or fostering in the future, keep reading! No one can be fully prepared for what comes ahead, but it's good to be as ready as you can.

Second, this book is for individuals and communities that care deeply about adoptive and foster families and want to support them in their journey. When I was a therapist providing counseling for kids in foster care and their families, I was shocked at the number of people who felt so alone. Many of these families were going through some very tough things with their kids, and the other people in their lives didn't seem to get it. Even their closest friends and family members who promised they would help and support them seemed to disappear when things got difficult. The church, which often encourages people to adopt and foster as an expression of God's love, is often nowhere to be found when families are struggling. This has to change.

Some of this lack of support has to do with a lack of information about foster care and adoption. If you aren't familiar with the unique challenges of those on this journey, it can be difficult to know how to engage with families who are struggling. If you don't have a basic knowledge of things like trauma, attachment, and sensory processing problems, it can be hard to know what is happening with the kids and families you love and want to support. If you aren't familiar with various parenting strategies for working with kids affected by adoption and foster care, it can be easy to judge parents who are doing things differently than you. So get informed! Read through this book and use the material to better support the adoptive and foster families in your life. Not everyone is called to adopt or foster, but we can all do something to help.

OUR STORIES

Let me take a moment to introduce myself and my coauthor. (For ease of reading, this book is written from my perspective, but the content reflects our collective experiences.) My name is Jenn, and I am originally from Canada. I moved to the United States to get my master's degree in clinical psychology at Wheaton College. After graduating, I worked as a therapist for kids in the foster care system. I counseled kids who were having a difficult time, and I also counseled foster parents and birth parents. During my years working as a therapist, I realized that many families were struggling because they didn't have enough support in their lives. They felt totally isolated and alone.

To meet the need for support, I started a ministry called Replanted. We organized monthly small groups for adoptive and foster families to develop relationships with people who understood the journey and what they were going through. We provided separate spaces for the adults and kids (with trained childcare mentors) so the adults could share a meal together, connect, and explore a topic (we produce a yearly discipleship curriculum for adoptive and foster parents) while the kids connected with each other, had fun, and discussed their own topics (we also produce a yearly kid's curriculum).

After a few years of hosting groups, Replanted became a nonprofit organization, and I started working with churches and organizations around the country to set up similar groups in different areas. Today, we have over thirty active small groups across fourteen states and two countries. We also host a national annual Replanted Conference, both in person and virtually, where adoptive and foster caregivers can come to be refreshed and equipped to better parent their kids. The conference is the highlight of my year, and I hear from many attendees that it's the highlight of theirs as well.

It is a privilege to write this book with my coauthor, Josh. He isn't just my coauthor—he is also my husband. We met through work—Josh is a licensed psychologist and professor of psychology at the University of North Texas. He has done extensive research and writing on positive psychology, religion/spirituality, and cultural humility. He is also a skilled writer and has joined me in my work with Replanted—which has been so much fun. And over the past few years it has been an adventure to enter into our own parenting journey together as well.

As a researcher, Josh has been helpful in making sure that the content we offer at Replanted and in this book is supported by research, and we have even done some research studies ourselves about issues related to adoption and foster parenting.

STORIES OF PARENTING IN ADOPTION AND FOSTER CARE
Parenting can be one of the most rewarding and meaningful activities of our lives, but it can also be one of the most

challenging. Throughout this book we will wrestle with how we can hold that tension. I invite you to think about where you are right now in your parenting journey. How are you feeling? Are things going pretty smoothly? Are you barely surviving? Somewhere in between?

Maybe you can connect with the story of Ben and McKenzie. They met in college and got married after graduation. They had always dreamed of having a big family, and they started trying to get pregnant in their mid-twenties. After several years of infertility, they decided to grow their family through adoption, and adopted a two-year-old boy named Timothy.

Fast-forward five years, and life is full! Ben and McKenzie adopted two additional children and now are a family of five—with three kids ranging in age from one to seven. As they have adjusted to their growing family, Ben and McKenzie have experienced some growing pains, particularly in their relationship with Timothy. He has started to act out at home and at school, talking back to his parents and getting in trouble with his teachers. He has also had some difficulties with learning, and he struggles to keep up with his peers. Ben and McKenzie aren't sure whether any of their struggles have to do with Timothy's being adopted, but they do wonder. Ben and McKenzie read somewhere that it's important to introduce adopted children to their culture of origin, but they don't really know how to do that. Timothy is Black. They live in a predominantly White community and attend a White church. Timothy hasn't talked much about being Black, but Ben and McKenzie wonder whether to bring it up and start the conversation. They know that just because he is not talking about it doesn't mean he is not thinking about it.

Or perhaps you can relate to the story of Maria. Maria is not married, and she loves kids and wanted to be a mom. She works as an elementary school teacher and has always had a heart for children who are struggling. Last year, she got her foster care license, and she recently started her first placement with a three-year-old girl named Eliza. Eliza was exposed to substances in utero, and she has had a difficult time connecting with Maria. She tends to stay by herself most of the time and is slow to warm up to people. Maria has tried all her normal strategies for connecting with young children, but nothing has seemed to work. Maybe it will just take time? Maria is also struggling because she doesn't know how long the foster placement will last. Eliza's biological parents want her back and are currently completing a drug rehabilitation program as part of their court-appointed plan for reunification. How attached should Maria get to Eliza? Maria wants to support the biological parents but is also angry with them for how they have hurt Eliza over the years. Sometimes Maria feels that Eliza would be better off with her, but she also knows that the ultimate goal of foster care is reunification. It's hard to know what to do with all her conflicting feelings.

Throughout this book, I will share several stories of adoptive and foster families. These are stories and issues from real families, although the names, identifying information, and some of the details have been changed for confidentiality. My hope is that you can see yourself in these stories—in their hopes and their challenges—and also experience grace and encouragement as you read. We're all in this together!

Wherever you are in your parenting journey, we are glad you are here. Whether you are just starting out (or thinking about it), or whether you are an adoption or foster care veteran, we hope this book will be helpful to you. Parenting children is one of the greatest privileges we can undertake. But it can be hard work! Sometimes it might seem like you can barely keep your head above water. The good news is, there is a baseline of knowledge and skills that can help prepare us for the journey. It still won't be easy—parenting never is. But it's good to be as equipped as possible.

DISCUSSION QUESTIONS

Our goal in this book is for you to actively engage with the material as you read. In fact, it would be great to read this book in community. It could be with your spouse and family, but it could also be with your friends or a small group. We weren't meant to do this parenting journey alone. As we end this first chapter, take some time to reflect:

- Where are you right now in your adoptive or foster care parenting journey? What feelings (e.g., sadness, anger, fear, happiness, excitement, tenderness) come up for you as you think about parenting?
- What is one of the main things you hope to gain from this book? What would make reading this book worthwhile?
- What is one of your main fears about reading this book? Do you have any concerns about trying to work on your parenting?

2

GOD'S HEART
FOR FAMILIES

As a Christian, I wholeheartedly believe that God loves families and kids. If a child doesn't have a place to belong or call home, God wants to provide that child with a safe place to heal, grow, and thrive. When marriages are broken or in distress, God wants to mend the broken places. And when families are struggling, God wants to bring healing and hope.

However, when you are parenting a child through adoption or foster care, your understanding of family tends to become more complex. The idealistic vision you had of what your family would look or be like may not match up with your experience. If you are a foster or adoptive parent, the composition of your family will likely shift and change over time, leading to periods of great joy and great sorrow. You might develop a relationship with your child's birth parents or siblings, expanding your definition of family even further—and adding even more complicated dynamics and emotions. With all of these complexities, what is God's heart for families? And how do we join in God's mission for our family?

LUCY AND TANNER

Lucy and Tanner both let out a sigh, sinking into their sofa after finally putting their nine-month-old foster son Grant to bed. They weren't sure how long sleep would last. Sleep was challenging for Grant. He had been in their home for about three months, and he had trouble settling down and relaxing. Bedtime was always an adventure.

Lucy was the one who had first thought about becoming foster parents. Growing up, she worked at youth summer camps and always loved working with kids. Lucy and Tanner had been trying to have kids for a while, and while they hadn't given up on having biological kids, Lucy felt some energy to try pursuing a different direction. There seemed to be a need for foster parents in their state, and it seemed like the perfect fit.

When they first decided to become foster parents, Lucy and Tanner had a variety of motivations. One was to love and serve kids in need. Another was to perhaps build their family through adoption (if it worked out). As you might imagine, their idea of what it meant for the foster care journey to "work out" shifted and changed throughout their experience.

Although both Lucy and Tanner say that becoming foster parents strengthened their faith in God, it also stretched and challenged them in ways they didn't expect. Specifically, it broadened their view of family and stretched their capacity to love.

When their caseworker first asked Lucy and Tanner about the possibility of welcoming Grant into their home, she told them the primary goal of this foster care placement would be reunification. Grant's birth mother Jacqueline was incarcerated, but she would be released from prison in a few months. Jacqueline wanted to be reunified with Grant, and said she was committed to doing everything it took to make that happen.

In that process, a shift happened for Lucy and Tanner. Instead of being focused on building their family, their perspective on their foster care journey changed. As they realized it was likely they would take care of Grant for only a limited time, they initially struggled with the uncertainty. But over time, they began to feel as if the uncertainty was okay—God was calling them to love and care for Grant for as long as he stayed in their home.

When Lucy and Tanner used to think about their "family," they thought about children staying with them permanently, either through adoption or by having biological kids. But Grant was part of their family, even though he would likely be reunified with his biological mother. They also felt that God was calling them to invite Jacqueline into the fold of their family. During Jacqueline's incarceration, Lucy started to write her letters regularly, and they began to develop a friendship. Lucy sent her pictures of Grant and updated her on what he was doing. Jacqueline was so grateful for this.

After Jacqueline was released from prison, Lucy and Tanner started supervised visits with her and Grant. This was challenging for everyone—Grant didn't recognize his birth mother and would run back to Lucy and Tanner for comfort. He would scream when they left the room, and their hearts would break. Over time, Grant started getting more connected to his birth mother, but you could see the confusion on his face when everyone was in the room. Sometimes it seemed like Jacqueline would take two steps forward and one step back as she readjusted to life outside. But this relationship definitely expanded their ability to love. Lucy would get frustrated with Jacqueline, who sometimes seemed to want their help and connection and other times seemed to resent them. But through the process, Lucy and Tanner realized that God was calling them to love Jacqueline as part of their family—never giving up on her, even when it seemed like that would be easier. Their situation might not have looked like the "traditional" family, but they were okay with that. Sometimes God's calling for our lives looks different from what we expected.

IN THE BEGINNING

What is God's heart for families and kids? We can start at the beginning in Genesis, where we see a description of the first family. (Don't worry about whether you believe the Genesis account is literal or not. At its heart, the Genesis account includes a description of God's views on family and relationships.) One key thing we learn from the Genesis account is that human beings were created in the image of God: "So God created mankind in his own image, in the image of God he created them; male and female he created them" (Genesis 1:27).

At the outset of this book, I want to affirm the deep sense of worth that God holds for all people. When we are parenting through adoption or foster care, it is easy to get frustrated and angry—at our child, at our child's birth family, at the judges and caseworkers, among others. When the frustration builds up, we can start to devalue some of these individuals, or think of them as "less than." It's important to remember that even on the most challenging days, that child (or adult) is made in the image of God.

Another thing we learn from the Genesis account is that it isn't good for human beings to be alone: "The LORD God said, 'It is not good for the man to be alone. I will make a helper suitable for him'" (Genesis 2:18).

We need to be careful not to put marriage on a pedestal. I love being married, but marriage doesn't happen or last for everyone. And there are so many single parents out there who are absolute rock stars. The broader point is we are meant to be in community with others. Life is hard. Parenting is hard. We need a support system if we are going to not only survive but thrive on this parenting journey. When we brought our daughter home, some of our friends had set up a meal train for us, and it was immensely helpful. Between the sleepless nights and figuring out how to be first-time parents, it was great to not have to think about what to prepare for dinner each night. It was also awesome to have friends check in on us to see how we were doing emotionally. Even though we had just welcomed a baby into our family and I knew I should feel so happy, I was experiencing so many more feelings than I expected—joy and excitement, yes, but also unexpected sadness at how our lives had drastically changed forever—and it was comforting to know we weren't alone in all those feelings.

We can also infer from the Genesis passage that it isn't good for kids to be alone. Children do best when they have a loving, stable family. When families break down and children are alone and without support, they tend to struggle. Adoption and foster care is holy work because it involves stepping into a child's aloneness and providing a stable family—either permanently or temporarily.

The third truth we learn from the creation account in Genesis is that it's good to have a family. God invites us to have kids: "God blessed them and said to them, 'Be fruitful and increase in number; fill the earth and subdue it'" (Genesis 1:28). Part of God's blessing involves family and children. Not everyone wants a family or kids, and that's okay. Deciding to have kids is a personal choice, and we also recognize that some people, for a variety of reasons, may be unable to have children. But for those of us who are involved in parenting (or hoping to be at some point), we can take heart. Being part of a family and having children are a big part of God's heart for us.

JESUS' WELCOME OF CHILDREN

Jesus never married or had kids. But throughout the Gospels, we see that Jesus placed a high value on children. For example, when the disciples asked who is the greatest in the kingdom of God, Jesus used children as his model:

> At that time the disciples came to Jesus and asked, "Who, then, is the greatest in the kingdom of heaven?"
>
> He called a little child to him, and placed the child among them. And he said: "Truly I tell you, unless you change and become like little children, you will never enter the kingdom of heaven. Therefore, whoever takes the lowly position of this child is the greatest in the kingdom of heaven. And whoever welcomes one such child in my name welcomes me." (Matthew 18:1–5)

In a society where children were often brushed aside and viewed as less important, Jesus made engaging with children a priority:

> Then people brought little children to Jesus for him to place his hands on them and pray for them. But the disciples rebuked them.
>
> Jesus said, "Let the little children come to me, and do not hinder them, for the kingdom of heaven belongs to such as these." When he had placed his hands on them, he went on from there. (Matthew 19:13–15)

Finally, Jesus placed a high priority on protecting children from harm. "If anyone causes one of these little ones—those who believe in me—to stumble, it would be better for them to have a large millstone hung around their neck and to be drowned in the depths of the sea" (Matthew 18:6). That verse is pretty harsh. And it is a verse that can be easy to resonate with when caring for children in foster care who have been abused and neglected. It's okay to feel righteous anger at what kids in foster care have experienced. But Jesus doesn't want us to stop there. The God of the universe loves us and wants us to be redeemed, healed, and fully restored. And the same is true for birth families trying to experience healing to restore their families. Jesus is cheering for all of us, no matter the outcome.

GOD'S HEART FOR ADOPTION AND FOSTER CARE

Most of the passages we have discussed so far are general in their description of God's heart for families and children. This is encouraging, but what about God's heart for adoption and foster care specifically? Is there anything we can take from Scripture about our specific situations?

First, there is a clear parallel between adoption and our relationship with God. Namely, even though we were separated from God because of our sin, we are adopted by God into God's family:

> For those who are led by the Spirit of God are the children of God. The Spirit you received does not make you slaves, so that you live in fear again; rather, the Spirit you received brought about your adoption to sonship. And by him we cry, "*Abba*, Father." . . . Now if we are children, then we are heirs—heirs of God and co-heirs with Christ, if indeed we share in his sufferings in order that we may also share in his glory. (Romans 8:14–17)

What a cool connection between how God views us and how we can view the children entrusted to us.

Also, throughout Scripture, there is a consistent importance placed on caring for those who are unable to care for themselves. James puts it this way: "Religion that God our Father accepts as pure and faultless is this: to look after orphans and widows in their distress and to keep oneself from being polluted by the world" (James 1:27). What better way to love others than to care for children who do not have a family or whose family is struggling?

When we hear this verse, we often think of "looking after orphans" as caring for children through adoption and foster care. But God is also asking us to aim higher. Understanding the love God has for families, caring for orphans should also include family preservation and support to keep families together when possible. For example, an organization called 1MILLIONHOME is doing amazing work internationally to help transition orphanages into family reintegration centers. Contrary to what most people believe, over 80 percent of children living in orphanages have at least one living parent.[1] We don't necessarily have an orphan crisis; we have a poverty crisis. Parents are choosing orphanages for their children because they know their children will be fed, educated, and clothed. They are choosing what they think is best for their child. But I sometimes wonder whether we underestimate the importance of a child's birth family to the child's well-being. For example, when children are separated from their family, they are at an increased risk of trauma and trafficking.[2] So what would it look like for us to live out James 1:27 in light of this reality?

The core teaching of Jesus isn't complicated. It all boils down to two main points: loving God and loving your neighbor. However, when Jesus said all the laws and commandments went back to loving God and loving your neighbor, the religious teachers wanted more information. The scripture says that one of the religious teachers "wanted to justify himself," so he asked Jesus who qualified as "neighbor" (Luke 10:29).

Jesus responded with perhaps his most famous parable, that of the good Samaritan. The story begins with a man being beaten by robbers and left for dead. A priest and a Levite, both members of the Jewish religious elite, see the man but walk past him on the other side of the road. Then a Samaritan, a man from a group of people the Jews considered enemies, sees the man, stops, and bandages his wounds. The Samaritan puts the man on his donkey, takes him to an inn, and pays for him to be taken care of.

Jesus concludes his teaching by asking his listeners who was a neighbor to the man who fell into the hands of robbers (Luke 10:36). The message of the parable is clear: Being a good neighbor involves loving and caring for people in practical ways. It doesn't matter that the Samaritan and the Jew were from different groups. We are called to love and serve those who are in need, regardless of where they come from.

The story of the good Samaritan has important implications for our work with adoption and foster care. Human beings have an innate drive to care for their biological offspring. But Jesus doesn't care much for these distinctions. When he was told his biological family wanted to speak with him, Jesus replied: "Who is my mother, and who are my brothers?" Then he pointed to his disciples and said, "Here are my mother and my brothers. For whoever does the will of my Father in heaven is my brother and sister and mother" (Matthew 12:48–50).

Jesus had a wider, more inclusive view of family. In this moment, he didn't make sharp distinctions about who is inside versus outside our call to love and serve. He considered his spiritual family to be just as important as (if not more so than) his biological family. What would it look like if we adopted this attitude in our own lives? How would our lives be transformed if we broadened our definition of family to include not only our adoptive and foster children but also our children's biological family?

DISCUSSION QUESTIONS

- How do you feel God views you in your adoption or foster care journey? Do you feel that God is proud, supportive, and pleased? Or do you feel that God is frustrated, angry, or judgmental? Or maybe something else?
- What do you think about God's heart for family and children? When you read the Bible, do you get the sense that God is rooting for you? What other verses or stories from Scripture motivate you in your parenting journey?
- How do you define family? Is there someone in your life who is frustrating and difficult to love? What might God be calling you to do in this relationship?

3

SELF-AWARENESS AND INFORMED EXPECTATIONS

Many books on parenting focus on children and their behaviors. Although this is important, we are going to start by looking at ourselves. Parenting is a relationship, and the most important tool you bring to the table is yourself. If you have spent much time around other families, you've probably realized that not everyone parents exactly the way you do. Some parents are more anxious; others are more laid-back. Some parents feel right at home with physical touch and nurturing, whereas others are more distant. Some parents are strict disciplinarians; others are more laissez-faire. And there are countless other aspects of parenting. Parenting styles aren't about "right" or "wrong." There is no one "right" style of parenting that always guarantees the desired outcome, although every parent always has room to grow.

When you think about these differences in parenting styles, where do you see yourself? If you had to describe yourself as a parent using a few sentences to note your most defining characteristics, what would you say? What are your areas of strength, and what areas could you improve? Take a moment right now to respond to these questions, either on paper or in your mind.

Just by reflecting on our parenting style, we have increased our self-awareness a little bit. That's more than most people do. Many of us operate on autopilot in many areas of our life—parenting included. We don't have a clear sense of why we do what we do—we just do what comes naturally to us. Now let's go one layer deeper. When you think about your parenting style, where do you think it came from? What helped shape and mold how you parent?

What came to mind for you? Maybe you thought about things like your cultural background or your religion. Perhaps you thought about a parenting class you took or a book you read. For many of us, however, the number one factor that influences our parenting is our own parents and how we were raised. We all grew up in a family, and certain norms and "ways of being" were shaped by how our parents engaged with us. We tend to do the same things with our own families, whether they are effective or not. Even if we learn something new about parenting, our go-to is usually related to how we were raised and what we experienced growing up. When we are under stress or don't have much bandwidth, we resort back to what we know.

For many of us, this "do what we know" parenting strategy happens more or less automatically, especially if we had an okay upbringing and there wasn't anything traumatic that made us question our experience. (If we had a very difficult upbringing, sometimes we will commit to doing the opposite of what we experienced growing up.) For example, I grew up on a farm in the country, and my family prided ourselves on being tough and being able to take care of ourselves. When my brother and I were growing up, there wasn't much space for being hurt or feeling sorry for ourselves—we were expected to suck it up and move on. And you got extra marks if you got really hurt and didn't cry. That was something to aspire to. I remember bragging with friends in high school about how long it had been since I had cried. And if you were one of those people who cried during a sad movie, you were weak. Now, I've done a lot of personal work, and hopefully I'm a little more balanced on this issue. But if I'm stressed or not thinking about it, I can have the attitude that my daughter should "suck it up" and be strong when she is hurt or struggling. When I'm in this place, I'm not as able to tune in to my daughter and meet her needs. I'm operating on autopilot.

Another common theme I experienced during childhood was that giving children attention when they were misbehaving or upset enabled their negative behavior. The view was that you should *always* ignore the negative behavior because the child was being manipulative. I now know this isn't helpful and usually isn't true, but it can be an easy default interpretation when I feel that my child is acting senselessly.

When you think of your parenting style, do you see any connection between your parenting style and the style of your primary caregivers growing up? Do you parent in a similar way or do the opposite of what you experienced as a child?

MICHAEL AND RHONDA

Michael and Rhonda had two older biological children—a nineteen-year-old son and a seventeen-year-old daughter. As their children had gotten older and grown more independent, Michael and Rhonda began to think God was leading them to open their family to more children through foster care. They got certified and received a placement of a sibling pair—Gary (age eight) and Devonte (age six).

Michael and Rhonda faced many challenges on their foster care journey, but one of the toughest challenges they faced was that although they had a set of "tried and true" parenting strategies they had used with their biological kids that worked well for them, these same strategies didn't seem to work with Gary and Devonte. This was difficult for Michael and Rhonda. They were open to trying new strategies, but it was still tough to make a shift in practice. It was challenging to recognize that the problem might be not with the kids, but the strategies.

A major area of frustration was correction and discipline. Michael and Rhonda had used time-outs with their biological children, and this had usually worked well. They also occasionally employed spanking with their biological children, but they were not allowed to spank their foster children. Michael and Rhonda's parenting expectation was that when an adult speaks, the children listen. Compliance is key. When they used this strategy with their biological children, the time-out gave the kids time away to settle themselves and reflect on their actions, but with Gary and Devonte, a time-out seemed to escalate their behavior. Michael and Rhonda found themselves having to up the ante and threaten to take away privileges, such as screen time and dessert. This also tended to escalate Gary's and Devonte's behavior, and Michael and Rhonda didn't know what else to do. They were stuck in a never-ending cycle, and soon Gary and Devonte didn't even care what privileges they lost.

Another struggle involved how Michael and Rhonda connected with their children. Michael and Rhonda were quite musical, and their biological children had been involved in band and choir growing up. Their family even had a band that performed sometimes at nursing homes and was quite the hit. Michael and Rhonda tried to include Gary and Devonte in the family music activities, but they didn't seem interested. Gary and Devonte were more interested in sports and basketball, which was new territory for Michael and Rhonda. They didn't have the experience, so it was difficult for them to connect in this way. It had seemed so easy to connect with their biological kids, but now everything seemed like a struggle. What was going on, and how could they bridge the gap?

PARENTING AND MEETING NEEDS

At its core, parenting is about meeting the needs of your child. Sometimes we are aware of our child's needs, and are willing and able to meet them. Other times, we aren't clear on what our child needs, and it's difficult to meet their needs. Or perhaps we have a good sense of what our child's needs are, but we are either unwilling or unable to meet them. Can you think of a time when you were able to recognize and meet one of your child's needs? What about a time when you did not recognize what your child needed? What about a time when you recognized your child's need but were unable or unwilling to meet the need?

We also have needs as parents. We might have a need for connection with our kids—maybe we need to feel loved or accepted by them. Or we might need a break or a sense of independence from our kids. We might have a need for our kids to listen *just one time* to a request and act immediately. Perhaps parenting helps us feel that we are doing something important or meaningful. If our kids look good and are well-behaved, it might reflect well on us.

Having needs is normal, and it's okay to have needs as parents. But sometimes the needs of our children conflict with our own needs. For example, maybe our child needs comfort and connection, but we need a break or compliance without an argument. Or maybe our child needs to develop a sense of independence and competence apart from us, but we need closeness and connection. Can you think of a time when your needs as a parent conflicted with one of your child's needs? How did you react in this situation?

On top of the general needs that all kids have, children who have been adopted or in foster care have unique needs. You may be parenting a child who has a history of trauma, experiences attachment difficulties, is working through a process of grief or loss, or is from another racial or ethnic background, to name a few. Some of these needs may be totally outside your experience because they weren't part of your history and upbringing. As an adoptive or foster parent, are you willing to learn new things and enter into your child's history and experience in order to meet their needs? Are you willing to step into the parts of you that get triggered and explore why?

What do you do when one of your child's needs conflicts with one of your needs as a parent? (And trust me, this will happen!) Ideally, the needs of your child should come first. But this is easier said than done. It's hard to meet your child's needs, especially when you are worn out and at the end of your rope. The more complete answer is that it's important to find creative ways to meet both your child's needs and your needs as a parent. You can put off your own needs for only so long before you start having a tough time. How might you work to meet both sets of needs? For example, if your child needs care or comfort and you need a break, could you meet your child's needs for comfort in the moment, and then take some time for self-care once your child goes down for a nap? Think about a situation where your child's needs conflicted with your own. Can you think of any creative solutions that might help meet both sets of needs, even if they seem contradictory on the surface?

MOTIVATIONS

Thinking about our motivations to engage in adoption and foster care can help us identify some of our needs as parents. Take a few minutes and reflect on what drove you to start the process of adoption and foster care. Why did you want to do it in the first place? For example, maybe you struggled with infertility and you viewed adoption and foster care as a way to build your family. Remember, your needs aren't wrong or bad, but it's important to be aware of your motivations and needs as you engage with your kids. For example, maybe you have a view of what a "family" should look like, and it could be challenging if your actual family deviates from the ideal picture in your mind. Or if your initial motivation to engage in foster care was to build your family, it might be tough for you to align with the goal of reunification, which is usually the primary goal in a foster care situation.

Another common motivation to engage in adoption or foster care involves one's faith. As we learned in the previous chapter, God has a tender heart for families, as well as for children who are struggling. Perhaps your faith motivates you to provide a family for a child. Again, this isn't a bad motivation, but it's important to keep this need in front of you. For example, you might have an expectation that if you are faithful and obedient to what God asked you to do regarding adoption and foster care, your family situation will "work out" (whatever that means to you). You might struggle with doubt or anger toward God if your family goes through a difficult time or if your child isn't healed from their physical or emotional challenges.

EXPECTATIONS

We all have expectations for our children. It's part of being a parent. Like our own needs, expectations aren't "bad" or "wrong," but we need to be aware of our expectations and hold them with care. And given our children's unique situations and needs, there may be times when our expectations are unrealistic. This can make our work more difficult as parents.

Parents often have high hopes for their children and many dreams for their kids' lives. This is a good thing, but again, be mindful of these expectations and hold them lightly, because they may be more about you than your child. For example, I played college basketball and loved competing at sports. I would be excited if my daughter loved sports, and I would really enjoy coaching and engaging with her in that way. This isn't a bad desire, but I need to hold my expectations and hopes for my daughter with an open hand. Sports may or may not reflect my kid's talents and interests. Am I able to hold my expectations lightly and follow the lead of my child instead?

ATTACHMENT NEEDS

Some of a child's most basic needs have to do with attachment. Attachment happens when your child develops a safe and secure connection with you as the parent. Children have two primary attachment needs: (1) the need for us to support their independence, and (2) the need for us to comfort them when they need help. There's a rhythm to it—back and forth, back and forth. In healthy attachment relationships, children use their parents as a secure base from which to explore, and can then return to their parents as a safe haven when they are scared or hurt or need support.

Our own personality and attachment history can affect the extent to which we can meet the attachment needs of our children. If we didn't have a secure attachment with our parents, we are likely to re-create an insecure attachment with our children. It's difficult to take a child to a place where we haven't gone ourselves. Even more difficult is that many of these attachment behaviors happen under the surface, on an unconscious level. If we haven't worked to gain awareness of our attachment tendencies and struggles, it is likely that we will pass on these tendencies to our children. Our attachment as a child translates into our ability to connect as an adult. If we want to have securely attached children, we need to explore our own attachment, because an adult with an insecure attachment style is less likely to raise a child who develops a secure attachment.[1] But the good news is, even when we are adults, our attachment styles can heal and grow.

I once watched a training on attachment called Circle of Security,[2] during which the speaker played a video clip of a beautiful landscape that overlooked the ocean. Calming music played in the background, and I remember feeling restful and at ease. I pictured myself relaxing and resting on an inner tube floating on the waves. Then he played the video clip again, except this time the music was dark and foreboding, like the soundtrack from the movie *Jaws*! That time, I had a completely different experience watching the video clip of the ocean landscape. Now I didn't want anything to do with the water—I pictured great white sharks swirling under its surface.

The speaker went on to make the point that parents can have very different reactions to their children and their needs because of their own upbringing and experiences with their own parents. For example, depending on their background and experiences, one parent might feel proud of their child venturing out to explore, whereas another parent might feel anxious. One parent might feel empathy and compassion when their child hurts themselves and needs support, whereas another parent might feel aggravated by the child's neediness. In these situations, the actions and needs of the child are the same, but parents have very different reactions because of their own experiences.

No one had a perfect upbringing or attachment experience with their parents. All our parents fell short in one way or another. It's impossible to perfectly meet a child's needs. Some of your needs as a child were not perfectly met. It's our job to work through that so we can better meet the needs of our children. This starts with recognizing that we all have some experiences and tendencies that make it difficult to meet the attachment needs of our children. The training called these tendencies our "shark music." When I watched the video clip at the training, the music influenced whether I felt relaxed and at ease thinking about the ocean or whether I felt scared. In a similar way, our own attachment experiences can influence our ability to interpret and meet the attachment needs of our children.

What is your "shark music"? What experiences shape how you interpret your child's attachment needs? What attachment needs of your children are most challenging for you to meet? If nothing comes to mind, it might be helpful to think about the two primary attachment needs: (1) the need to support the child's independence, and (2) the need to care for and comfort the child when they need us. Which need is most difficult for you to meet? Can you think about anything from your upbringing that might relate to your challenges in meeting the attachment needs of your child?

DISCUSSION QUESTIONS

- What stuck out to you most as you read this chapter? Was there anything that you realized about your parenting style that was a new understanding for you?
- What connections do you notice between your upbringing and relationship with parents and your parenting style and relationship with children?
- What are your strengths when it comes to meeting the needs of your children? What are your weaknesses or areas for growth?

Part II

KNOWLEDGE

4

LANGUAGE MATTERS

The words and language we use with our families have great power, both to build up and to tear down. When I was little, I was taught the rhyme "Sticks and stones can break my bones, but words can never hurt me." Looking back, I understand the intent—my parents and teachers were trying to help me be resilient when I had to face the mean words and put-downs from other children at school and on the playground. But it wasn't true. Throughout my growing-up years, I learned that words had the potential to hurt . . . a lot!

I also remember hearing certain words and phrases tossed off by other kids—or even adults—without much thought to the powerful underlying message they conveyed. When a boy didn't know how to throw a baseball at gym class, someone would ridicule him by saying, "You throw like a girl!" What was the underlying message behind this comment? Not only did it imply that "throwing like a girl" was something that boys shouldn't do, but it also communicated that girls (like me) couldn't throw a baseball well. Phrases like this made me mad as a kid because I was a girl *and* I loved to play baseball— and I was good at it. I didn't want to be put into the box those words created. My classmates may not have intended to send that message to me, but that was the impact their words had.

In a similar way, paying attention to our language is critical when parenting our kids, especially in the context of parenting through adoption and foster care. Many of these ideas might be new for you, and that's okay. If you find yourself using some of the language I recommend thinking about more critically in this chapter, don't be too hard on yourself. Many of the examples in this chapter are subtle, and most of the parents who use this type of language are well-intentioned. But if you're willing, be open to some of the underlying meanings of some common words or phrases that we tend to use as parents.

To begin, let's do a brief exercise. Below is a list of common words or phrases that adoptive and foster parents sometimes use. For each one, reflect on what some of the underlying meanings might be. If you're reading this book with your spouse or a small group, feel free to discuss and share your initial thoughts about the meanings of each of the words. We'll explore more about the messages communicated by each word or phrase as we move forward.

- "Orphan"
- "Vulnerable children"
- "Children from hard places"
- "Adoption rocks."
- "Love makes a family."
- "God chose you for our family."
- "Adoption party"
- "I don't see color."

JOANNE AND TOM

Joanne and Tom were so excited they could hardly contain themselves. Ever since they began dating and got married, they had wanted kids. Joanne in particular also had a huge heart for adoption and foster care. Her parents had adopted her baby brother, so adoption was always part of their family story. Joanne loved the idea of providing a safe and loving home for a child who didn't have access to one.

Their first foster placement was a three-year-old boy named Roger, and he stayed with Joanne and Tom for a little less than a year. Eventually, Roger was reunited with his birth mother. Joanne and Tom had so many feelings about this. On one hand, they had known going into the placement that the primary goal was reunification, so they were so happy that Roger's mother did what she needed to do so they could be together again. However, they also felt a tremendous sadness. Roger was part of their family, and saying goodbye to him was devastating. They missed his giggles, playing tag in the backyard, and the snuggles at bedtime. Would they ever see him again? Would he even remember them?

Their second foster placement was a five-year-old boy named Damen. Damen's situation was different from Roger's—although the primary goal of the placement was still reunification, the foster agency had informed Joanne and Tom that the birth family would likely be unable to do what was needed to be done to get Damen back. This was difficult for Joanne and Tom. Although they wanted to respect the birth parents and cheer for their healing, it was tough not to also hope that they could eventually adopt Damen.

After about a year and a half, the judge terminated the parental rights of the birth parents, and Joanne and Tom were given the opportunity to adopt Damen into their family. Not having had the celebrations that often accompany a biological birth, such as a baby shower or "gender reveal party," Joanne and Tom wanted to invite their family and close friends over to have an "adoption day party." Many of these family members and friends had grown close to Damen over the past year and a half, and they were excited to celebrate with Joanne, Tom, and Damen.

When the day of the party came, Damen refused to come out of his room and join the party. Joanne and Tom tried to ask Damen what he was feeling and why he was sad and angry, but Damen wouldn't respond. He just stayed in his room. Finally, Joanne and Tom got Damen to come downstairs, but he stayed in the corner looking sullen and angry. Joanne and Tom ended the party early, not sure what was going on with Damen.

Later on, in counseling, Damen confided to his counselor that the "adoption day party" was one of the saddest days of his life. Even though he loved Joanne and Tom, he had always secretly hoped to be able to go back home and be with his birth mom and dad and younger sister. When Joanne, Tom, and the judge told him he was adopted, he realized this meant he was never going back to his biological family. Everyone around him was celebrating and happy, but this wasn't Damen's experience. It wasn't that he was ungrateful or didn't love Joanne and Tom. But his feelings were mixed. He also felt mad at his birth parents. Did they not care about him? Why wouldn't they do what they needed to be a family again? He certainly wasn't in the mood to have a party that day.

LANGUAGE REFLECTS AND CREATES REALITY

Language is important because it reflects our reality. In other words, the language we use reflects our beliefs, values, and attitudes. Sometimes it can even be a window into beliefs, values, and attitudes we may not even realize we have. In the example above, what do you think using the language of "adoption day party" said about Joanne and Tom's beliefs, values, and attitudes? It may have reflected an attitude that adoption is something great and worth celebrating. This attitude isn't wrong per se—adoption *can* be great and worth celebrating. And for some children, they have longed for the day when they would be adopted by a family who loves them. So yes, an adoption party might be something they are fully in support of. The potential problem was that Joanne and Tom did not fully consider Damen's experience of the adoption, and they weren't able to connect with or honor the pain and grief he felt around cutting ties with his birth family.

It can be helpful to spend some time observing and reflecting on the language you use about adoption and foster care, as well as the language used by those around you. What does your language say about your underlying beliefs, values, and attitudes, specifically about adoption, foster care, or your family? What has shaped those word choices? Whose experience or perspective might be missing from or diminished or contradicted by the language you use? This practice could give you insight into underlying attitudes you didn't even know you had. For example, if you share with people that you are hoping to "foster to adopt," that could communicate to your child that you hope they don't reunify with their birth family and instead stay with you. How might that affect their relationship with you? It's good to keep these attitudes in front of you because our language communicates our underlying attitudes to those around us, whether we are aware of these attitudes or not.

Language not only reflects our reality but can *create* our reality. This is especially true about the language we use when we are with our kids. Our children are like sponges, still developing their beliefs, values, and attitudes. When we use language that reflects our attitudes, these same attitudes can be "caught" by our children.

At the beginning of the chapter, I shared about how when I was younger, I would get frustrated when people used the phrase "throw like a girl" in a negative or disparaging way. And I continue to get frustrated by this type of language today. Children are malleable. If a girl is told (even indirectly) that she can't throw a baseball well because of her gender, she may believe it, and be less likely to work to improve her ability. After all, why try to improve something if it won't do any good?

Again, the key is to be aware of the language we use and how it might affect our children. What underlying message is our language sending to our kids? Is this a message we want to send? What impact might this message have on our children? Is it empowering or disempowering? Is it about my needs, desires, and wants, or does it reflect theirs? The rest of this chapter walks through some of the key categories of language related to adoption and foster care so we can think critically about the underlying messages they send to those around us. Remember, language has a powerful impact. We influence our children through the words and messages we tell them every day. As much as possible, let's keep this in front of us and use our language to build others.

LANGUAGE ABOUT ADOPTION AND FOSTER CARE IN GENERAL

To begin, let's consider how we talk about adoption and foster care generally. There are two common, important kinds of language to consider. The first is language that frames adoption and foster care in an overly positive, enthusiastic manner, without considering the other side of the coin. For example, many people talk about how "adoption rocks!" or "adoption is amazing!" Like Joanne and Tom, parents will often throw adoption parties or have celebrations marking the anniversary of when their child's adoption became official.

It is important to proceed cautiously here, because I understand having a positive view of adoption and foster care. It is very close to the heart of God, some children need families, and I *do* believe it is worthy of celebration. I love to see families come together and children celebrated, honored, and loved. However, for many of our kids, their experience of adoption and foster care placement is mixed. The joy and happiness of a new home and family are often mixed with grief and loss of what they have had to leave behind. Becoming a permanent member of an adoptive family means they will never be with their birth family. For an adoptee or foster child, does adoption rock? Maybe, maybe not. Using overly positive language and not respecting the full range of feelings and experiences a child is going through can be invalidating. Instead, try to put yourself in your child's shoes—ask your child about their experience, and use language that reflects the full range of their experience. As Ferera Swan, an adult adoptee who is now a recording artist and an activist for adoptee rights and adoption reform, has said, "An adoptive couple's dream come true is an infant's worst nightmare."[1] Families were never meant to be broken or split apart. Can the language we use help us hold that loss with our kids?

The second kind of language to consider is when parents talk about their experience with adoption and foster care in difficult or traumatic terms. I often hear parents use war metaphors, comparing adoptive or foster parenting to a "battle," "war zone," or living "in the trenches." This language can paint our experience with our children in an overly negative light, and frames our child's behavior or presence as a source of irreparable harm or trauma.

Again, it is important to proceed cautiously here, because for many parents, this type of language can feel like an accurate reflection of their experiences. Many parents are going through incredibly difficult times with their children. Also, everyone needs a place to vent and be honest and vulnerable about what is going on in their lives. We need to have spaces where we can let our hair down and be our true, raw selves without needing to edit or clean up our language. In fact, one of the primary goals of the Replanted small groups and conference is to provide parents and caregivers with a safe space to be totally vulnerable with one another in a community of others who really get it. But if we speak about our adoption or foster care experience in an overly negative way around our children or in public spaces, we can communicate to our kids that they are hurtful toward us or have caused us irreparable damage. This can add guilt and shame to a child's already challenging experience. So find spaces to vent without editing, but carefully consider the language you use around your kids or in public.

Just as parents need spaces to be vulnerable and honest, so do our kids. Kids affected by adoption and foster care need to relate with others who understand their experience—they need spaces where they can expose their deepest longings, questions, heartaches, and hopes. Connect your child with other kids in similar situations or with adult adoptees and foster alumni. At our Replanted Conference, we give attendees "same here" paddles to hold up when someone expresses a feeling or experience they relate to, and I love watching attendees look around the room and realize they are not alone. There is something so connecting when you share your story or experience and someone says, "Same here—I know what you're going through." The same is just as true for our children.

LANGUAGE ABOUT OUR CHILDREN

Let's look at some of the language we use to describe our children. As a helpful guide, we can look to the principle of "person first" language, pioneered by those in the disability community to emphasize putting a person before their category. For example, whereas "foster child" centers the state of being in foster care, "child in foster care" centers the child. A person-first alternative to "my special needs child" would be "my child with an FASD diagnosis." Using person-first language is a more accurate and respectful way of speaking about our children, and it makes it less likely for us and others to rely on stereotypes because the child themself is the primary focus—the category the child belongs to is simply one descriptor of the child.

It's also important to consider how we use the word *orphan* to refer to children who are adopted or in foster care. We use the terms *orphan* and *orphan care* quite a bit in the adoption and foster care community, especially when talking about international adoption. For Christians, this language connects us to the many Bible passages referencing orphans, such as James 1:27, which says, "Religion that God our Father accepts as pure and faultless is this: to look after orphans and widows in their distress. . . ." However, the word *orphan* has a specific meaning—it refers to a child whose parents have died. But most children who live in orphanages are not actually orphans—one report estimates that 80 percent of children living in institutional care have one or both living parents.[2]

It's important to be accurate with our language because the words we use to describe our children's reality influence our responses to that reality and what we think should be done moving forward. For example, if a child's parents have died, it makes sense to have the child be adopted by a family who can care for them. However, if the child has a living parent and the child is living in institutional care for another reason—for example, poverty, or the parent not being able to care for the child's medical needs—a different solution may be prioritized (e.g., more social and family support).

We must also use caution when lumping children in foster care under the "orphan care" umbrella. I have worked with many children in foster care who feel hurt by this terminology because it belittles their birth families and who and where they come from. Some Christians may use the term *orphan care* to connect with the broad biblical mandate to care for children who need a home, for any reason or any length of time. This connection may not be a bad thing, in spirit. However, using this type of language may have unintended consequences, both for the children themselves and for those seeking solutions.

Another way we can do better with language is to follow our child's lead. For example, it can be hard to know whether to refer to a child's birth family as the child's birth family, first family, family of origin, or so on. When in doubt, ask your child what they prefer and follow their lead. By allowing the child to choose the language they would like to use to identify the people in their life, we can empower them and create space for the range of feelings and emotions they may be experiencing. This is also true when it comes to how children identify us (as parents), which can be especially complicated for children in foster care. A little boy I worked with in foster care told me his foster parents wanted him to call them Mom and Dad. However, in his eyes he already had a mom and dad, and using that language for his foster parents was not true to his experience. When you follow your child's lead, you honor their experience and allow them to define the terms according to their comfort level. For some children, using Mom or Dad feels appropriate because that is who you are to them. However, for other children, Mom or Dad is a sacred title—they may want to protect it, and they may need time and trust to develop before they feel safe to use it. For some children, using Mom and Dad for someone other than their birth parents may feel like a betrayal, and they may never feel ready to use it for anyone else. Sit with them in those emotions and do not force them to use language they have not chosen themselves.

How can we have these conversations with our kids? Here are some scripts I recommend using:

- A good place to start is with a basic introduction: "My name is Ms. Jenn. I'm glad to meet you. I know you must be feeling a lot of things right now, and I want you to know, all those feelings are okay." (When children are feeling overwhelmed, remember to keep it simple. Introduce yourself by your name and keep it at that. They may change what they call you over time. Follow their lead.)

- For children who need options: "It's okay if you don't know what to call me. Here are some ideas: Ms. Jenn, Ms. Hook, Mama Jenn, Mom, Auntie Jenn, or Ms. Awesome-sauce." (Being playful often disarms fear.) "Would you like to pick one of those? And I want you to know, if you change your mind about what you'd like to call me, that is okay!"

- "You will always be part of our family, whether you're with us for a short time or a long time." (Validate any feelings they might be experiencing.) "While you are here, what would you like to call us?"

One last type of language to consider is how we describe children who have been adopted or are in foster care, specifically related to the challenging circumstances they have been through or the trauma they may have experienced. For example, we sometimes use phrases such as "vulnerable children" or "children from hard places" to describe kids who have been adopted or are in foster care. Again, it is important to proceed cautiously here, because these phrases are often accurate descriptions of a child's situation. But phrases like this focus on the negative aspects of our child's history or experiences. Sometimes it is helpful to acknowledge the painful and difficult aspects of our child's experiences, but the danger with this kind of language is that we can forget our child is a multifaceted human being with a wide range of challenges and strengths and resiliencies. When we constantly focus on the negative side of the equation, we can miss some of the important positive strengths that our child brings to the table.

LANGUAGE ABOUT BIRTH FAMILIES

Next, let's talk about the language that we use to describe our child's birth family. Navigating the relationship with a child's birth family can be challenging and can bring up many uncomfortable feelings and emotions. Also, there are likely nuances to be considered because of your particular situation, such as whether the adoption is open or closed or the extent to which the birth family is safe. However, if we believe, as I do, that God wants to preserve and repair broken families, the language we use should help us engage in the work of family reunification whenever it is safe and possible.

Using language that is respectful of your child's birth family can be challenging, especially if the birth family is doing things or making choices that are harmful to you or your children. Conversely, it can be easy to make critical or disparaging remarks about your child's birth family, even in the presence of your child. As much as possible, try to avoid doing this. Again, we all need a place to vent and be completely raw, so it's a good idea to have a small group where you can be vulnerable. But when we are in the presence of our children or in public, we should think critically about the language we use when talking about a child's birth parents.

As your children grow and develop, they will begin to think critically about their birth families and what you have communicated about them. If your language has been negative—for example, talking about how your child's birth parents are "terrible people" or "lowlifes who are addicted to drugs"—what does that say about your child who shares their DNA? Your child will *always* be connected to their birth family, whether you want them to be or not, and whether they are actively in relationship with them or not. Allow your child to form opinions and views about their birth family without influencing their narrative. Support the goal of reunification if possible. Their views will likely shift and pivot multiple times, and our job as parents is to validate and support them through all the ups and downs of that process.

All people are worthy of love and respect, regardless of their choices or the mistakes they have made. This is the heart of the gospel—even though we sin and make mistakes, God loves us and wants to be in relationship with us even when it comes at a great cost (e.g., this is modeled in God's sending Jesus to us, and Jesus' willingness to demonstrate love even to the point of dying on the cross). No one is "too far gone" to be outside the reach of God's love and desire for reconciliation. If we truly want to model Jesus to the world around us, we should have the same attitude toward other people in our lives, including our child's birth parents. If we believe that God loves us and pursues us despite all the ways we mess up, and if we are called to love like God, then that must include birth families who have made mistakes.

What does this look like practically? Avoid making negative or disparaging remarks about your child's birth parents when you are around your child or in public. When you need to communicate challenging or difficult information about your child's birth parents, do so in a kind and age-appropriate manner. Remember, you can be honest about a person's behaviors and the consequences of those behaviors yet still be kind and loving toward that person. It can also be helpful to remember times when we have needed grace and forgiveness. God has given us massive amounts of grace over the years—can we in turn give grace to those in our lives who are difficult to love?

LANGUAGE ABOUT CULTURAL DIFFERENCES

The final category is the language we use around culture and cultural differences. Culture is a broad term that describes our beliefs, attitudes, values, traditions, and ways of being in the world. We develop our cultural background as we grow up and are influenced by a variety of sources, such as our families, neighborhoods, schools, and religious institutions. Numerous cultural identities can influence our upbringing and development, including race, ethnicity, nationality, language, gender, religion, sexual orientation, and socioeconomic status.

Many adoptive and foster families are made up of members who do not share the same cultural identities. This diversity of culture in the same family can be interesting and vibrant, but it can also bring challenges and difficulties. Families can experience growing pains as they explore how to develop a family system that works together.

The language we use about culture often reflects our attitudes. In a model of intercultural competence, Mitchell

Hammer, Milton Bennett, and Richard Wiseman describe various ways of engaging with cultural differences.[3] First, people sometimes fail to notice cultural differences (denial). They might notice superficial differences like skin color and food preferences, but they fail to understand cultural differences at a deeper level, such as beliefs, values, attitudes, and preferences.

Second, people sometimes notice cultural differences, but judge them as good or bad (polarization). We might criticize another cultural group, perhaps relying on stereotypes. On many cultural issues (e.g., protests over systemic racism, LGBTQ issues, immigration), people fall into an "us versus them" mentality, deciding their own position and then heavily criticizing and villainizing those on the other side. (Having convictions about issues that affect us or others can be important and valuable. But it is also important to engage with others who are different in ways that we would like to be treated.)

Third, people sometimes try to de-emphasize cultural differences and focus on the things we have in common (minimization). This is reflected in phrases such as "I don't see color" or "We are all part of the human race." Minimization can be common among Christians who want to de-emphasize culture and focus on our identity in Christ. Yes, our identity in Christ is important and something that bonds us together; however, can we also appreciate and respect our cultural differences? Minimization can often deny people's lived experience because people experience important differences in the ways they are treated because of their cultural identities.

The final two ways of engaging cultural differences, acceptance and accommodation, are usually more effective in relationships where cultural differences are present. Acceptance involves truly valuing and respecting cultural differences and being open and curious to someone with a different perspective.

Humility is a big part of acceptance—we don't see our cultural viewpoint as the one right way of seeing the world. Accommodation goes a step further and involves being willing to change or adjust our way of being in and seeing the world to help make others feel more comfortable. This is very challenging but critically important when we parent children from a different cultural background. We will talk more about how to do this in a later chapter, but for now, reflect on how you talk about culture and cultural differences and what your language might say about how you engage with such differences.

DISCUSSION QUESTIONS

- What stuck out to you most as you read this chapter? How have you experienced the power of language to both reflect and create our reality? How do you understand it differently now?
- When you practiced paying attention and taking notice of the language you use, what came up for you? What was one thing you noticed about your language that you weren't aware of before?
- What is one thing you want to change or adjust about your language moving forward?

5

TRAUMA AND ITS IMPACT

When parenting children through adoption and foster care, it is critical to understand the role of trauma and how it affects our children (and how it can affect us). When I worked as a counselor for kids in foster care, hearing about their experiences of trauma was the most difficult part of my job. My heart broke for the kids and what they had been through. Many of the children I worked with saw or experienced things that no kid should have to endure. These experiences were not their fault, and they had no control over what happened to them. And yet their trauma experiences shaped who they were and affected so many aspects of their lives, from their thoughts and emotions to their behaviors and relationships. For these kids to experience healing, it was important to understand what had happened to them.

It was also important for parents to understand their child's trauma experiences. I worked with parents as well as kids, and sometimes parents came to me flabbergasted by their child's behaviors. Their kids did things like hoarding food, breaking objects, and engaging in provocative sexual play. Some parents were at their wit's end, not knowing how to respond to behavior that seemed so unusual and outside the bounds of what was expected. Many parents saw their child's behavior as willful, defiant, or disrespectful; however, it's important to view these behaviors through a trauma lens. For the parents, too, understanding the effects of trauma was key. It didn't necessarily solve the problems they were experiencing—there was still a long road ahead for many of the families I worked with. But it did increase empathy and understanding once parents could connect the dots between the trauma their children experienced and their current behaviors. Usually, the parents didn't think they were losing their wits anymore, which counted for something.

Many of us have the misconception that adoption or foster care heals trauma. But that is not accurate. Rev. Keith Griffith is commonly quoted as saying, "Adoption loss is the only trauma in the world where the victims are expected by the whole of society to be grateful." No adoption is void of trauma. I like the way adoptee Jada Bromberg has put it: "Being adopted didn't give me a better life, but it changed the route of my journey."[1] All adopted persons and foster alumni live with separation trauma—they were separated and disconnected from their birth family, and for some children in foster care, they were separated from a foster family they loved. For them, "healing" doesn't mean their trauma or experiences are resolved—that separation will always be a loss they feel on some level. Healing is a lifelong process that ebbs and flows over time. Random things can trigger trauma and loss experiences. It will always be part of their story. Adoptees and foster alumni will always carry those scars, and if we want to journey with them toward healing, we must enter those spaces with them with humility and compassion.

ERIN

Erin was a thirty-year-old single mom who adopted her niece Kim from the foster care system when she was six years old.

Erin never intended to be a foster or adoptive parent, but her sister was addicted to drugs, and when her niece went into foster care, she agreed to adopt her. By the time Kim was placed with Erin, she had already experienced several traumatic things. To begin with, she was exposed to drugs and alcohol in utero. Sometimes we don't think about things that happen before a child is born as traumatic events, but trauma can refer to anything that is physically or emotionally harmful or threatening and can have lasting effects on a person's functioning and well-being. It doesn't matter when it happens—trauma can occur even before a child is born.

Kim's mother struggled to adequately meet Kim's basic needs when she was a baby—which is called neglect. Also, Kim's mother had a series of boyfriends who came in and out of the home when Kim was young. One of the boyfriends sexually abused Kim, which was the event that led to the Department of Child and Family Services removing Kim from her home—more trauma.

Kim was placed in two foster care homes while they worked to find a kinship placement for her. Although Kim was now in a safe home environment, she was very sad that she could not go home to her birth mother, and she didn't understand the permanence of what had happened. Her birth mother continued to struggle with drugs and alcohol, among other difficulties, so Kim was not able to see her birth mother for quite some time. As we will discuss later, the experience of separation, loss, and grief can be traumatic for children who are adopted or in foster care.

As Kim grew up, her trauma manifested in several ways. For example, she exhibited multiple emotional and behavioral problems as a child. When Erin corrected her or gave a consequence, Kim would become irate, yelling, screaming, and sometimes even throwing things around the house and at Erin. When she became a teenager, Kim started to experiment with drugs and alcohol. She ended up failing eighth grade, which prompted Erin to get Kim into counseling. Sometimes the counselor met with Kim individually, and sometimes the counselor met with Kim and Erin together. In counseling, one of the things Kim and her counselor discussed was the trauma Kim experienced, particularly the abuse from her birth mother's boyfriend.

Kim is still struggling, and the future is uncertain. There aren't easy fixes when kids have gone through very difficult circumstances. Still, counseling helped Erin understand Kim's history of trauma and a bit about what Kim had been through. Erin began to see connections between Kim's trauma history and her acting-out behaviors. And Erin was able to understand and talk about her own experiences of vicarious trauma in parenting Kim and receive support for that.

WHAT IS TRAUMA?

Trauma, as noted earlier, is a broad term that refers to something that is physically or emotionally threatening or harmful and has long-term effects on a person's physical or emotional health and well-being. Kids can experience different types of trauma, including abuse (whether physical, sexual, emotional), neglect, exposure to drugs or alcohol in utero, serious medical challenges, poverty, separation from loved ones, bullying, witnessing harm to a loved one, experiencing or witnessing natural disasters or accidents, unpredictable parental behavior (such as a parent who struggles with an addiction or mental illness), being in the child welfare system, and being the target of racial prejudice or discrimination.[2]

When we think about the significance of trauma in our children's lives, it is important to recognize that children can experience trauma differently than adults. I have met some parents who downplay their children's experiences of trauma, especially if the child didn't experience something the parent would label as "extremely serious," such as abuse or neglect. Parents often feel this way when they bring a child into their home at birth—they see their child as starting with a clean slate, as though whatever happened in the womb or the separation from their birth family has no impact if the child cannot consciously remember it. It's as if parents put themselves in their child's shoes and think, "That experience wasn't *that* bad. I don't understand why my child is struggling so much." But we must remember that as adults, we have more highly developed coping resources than our children. The same event can be experienced by people differently depending on their capacity to cope. It's important to acknowledge our child's experience for what it is, without trying to downplay or modify it. When it comes to trauma, the important thing is how our children experienced it, not how we judge the experience from an adult point of view. We should never create a trauma hierarchy. That invalidates our children's experience.

THE IMPACT OF TRAUMA

Some level of stress and challenge is good and adaptive for children. When my daughter was learning to walk, for example, she would lose her balance and fall multiple times a day, which sometimes led to a high degree of frustration and crying. But this was essential to her process of learning to walk. As children grow up, they encounter difficulties and challenges relative to their developmental level. This is good and normal. Usually, with adequate support, children are able to meet the various challenges they face and build competence and confidence as they go.

But trauma is different. When children experience trauma, they are faced with something so terrible or extreme that it overwhelms their ability to cope. The traumatic event activates a fight, flight, or freeze response, which can affect children's bodies, brains, emotions, and behavior. (Researchers have recently noted a possible fourth response to trauma called the fawn response, where victims respond to trauma by trying to appease or please the threatening person.[3]) Children who have experienced trauma learn at a subconscious level that they can't trust others to meet their needs and can trust only themselves. So even if your child is eight years old, they may be functioning at the emotional level of a four-year-old with the street smarts of a sixteen-year-old. Trauma affects the brain and behavior.

Here are some of the most common effects of trauma in each of these areas:[4]

- The physical impact of trauma can include difficulties controlling responses to stress, as well as chronic illness or health issues (e.g., heart disease, obesity), even into adulthood.
- The impact of trauma on children's brains can include difficulties with thinking, learning, concentrating, memory, and switching from one task to another. Trauma affects three main parts of the brain: the amygdala, hippocampus, and prefrontal cortex.[5] In people who have experienced trauma, the amygdala, which involves emotions and survival, can take over, suppressing the prefrontal cortex, which is responsible for emotional regulation and impulse control. This is why children can be in dysregulated states for prolonged periods. The hippocampus, which is responsible for memory, is

also affected—events that trigger memories of traumatic events can be perceived as threats themselves.[6]

- The emotional impact of trauma can include low self-esteem; feeling unsafe; difficulty regulating emotions, forming attachments to caregivers, and developing friendships; trust issues; depression; and anxiety.
- The impact of trauma on children's behavior can include lack of impulse control, fighting, aggression, running away, substance misuse, and suicide.

The effects of trauma are broad. It is difficult to predict how a child will react to a traumatic experience. But developing awareness of some of the common ways that trauma can affect a child's experience can help you better understand and help your child. For example, a family I worked with once told me that every time their child got in the car, he would have a massive fit. He would scream, cry, and become dysregulated (struggle to control his emotions) for a long time. I asked them why a car might be triggering for their child. After they thought about it, a lightbulb went off. They shared that when he was removed from his birth mother's care, he was placed in a stranger's car (the caseworker) and taken away from his mother. He screamed, thrashed, and tried to get out. He cried out for his birth mom as they drove away. So every time he got in a car, it reminded him of being taken from his birth mother. Plus, there might be an association that getting in cars meant he might be taken from the people he knew and loved. For him, cars weren't safe. They were traumatic.

How a potentially traumatic experience will affect a child is not clear-cut. Some children may not experience long-term negative effects of a traumatic event, whereas a similar event may have dramatic long-term effects for other children. Here

are some of the key factors that can contribute to the impact
of a traumatic event:[7]

- Age: In general, younger children who experience a
  traumatic event will likely experience more symptoms
  than older children who experience a traumatic event.
- Frequency: If a child experiences a traumatic event multiple times, or experiences multiple types of traumatic
  events, they will likely experience more symptoms than
  if they experience a single instance of trauma.
- Relationships: Children with healthy relationships in
  their lives (with parents, teachers, coaches, pastors
  or other religious leaders) are more likely to recover
  from a traumatic experience than children who are
  more isolated.
- Coping skills: Children with more well-developed coping skills are more likely to recover from an experience
  of trauma than children with fewer coping skills in their
  repertoire. Coping skills can be broadly divided into two
  categories: problem-focused coping strategies attempt to
  deal practically with the source of the problem, whereas
  emotional-focused coping strategies (e.g., journaling,
  counseling, prayer) attempt to deal with the distress that
  comes up because of the situation.
- Perception: How the child interprets the traumatic event
  affects the impact of the trauma. For example, how
  dangerous, threatening, or uncontrollable did the child
  perceive the traumatic event to be?
- Sensitivity: The personality and disposition of the child
  plays a role when determining the impact of the traumatic
  event. Some children are more sensitive than others.

- Community: A child can be harmed by risk factors in their community, including high rates of violence or crime, high rates of unemployment, easy access to drugs, and an unstable house environment (such as one where residents move frequently or don't know to look out for each other), and others. Conversely, community protective factors include having access to medical care, mental health services, safe and stable housing, economic and financial help, and after-school activities; strong connections between residents; high levels of community involvement; no tolerance for violence, among others.[8]

When a child has a severe reaction to a traumatic event, the child may develop symptoms of post-traumatic stress disorder. Three core groups of symptoms are associated with PTSD.[9] The first group of symptoms involves reexperiencing the trauma in some way, such as intrusive recollections of the experience, flashbacks, nightmares, repetitive play, or trauma reenactment. Reminders of the trauma (e.g., people, places, other stimuli) can cause high levels of distress. Memories are often intimately connected to sights, smells, and sounds. Even in your own experience, for example, you might smell a cologne or perfume at a restaurant that reminds you of a loved one and a memorable date or experience you shared together. The same can be true of smells that remind us of painful experiences—a sense memory can bring us right back into the moment and the way we felt then.

The second group of symptoms involves avoidance of trauma reminders and emotional numbing, including symptoms such as efforts to avoid trauma reminders, inability to recall some aspect of the trauma, decreased interest in formerly enjoyable activities, detachment from others, restricted affect, and a sense of the future being shorter than before.

The third group of symptoms involves hyperarousal, such as difficulty sleeping, reckless behavior, irritability or angry outbursts, difficulty concentrating, hypervigilance, and increased startle reaction. I worked with a girl who struggled in school for this very reason. At face value, it appeared she just couldn't focus or concentrate at school, leading teachers to believe she had ADHD. But for this girl, trauma memories flooded her brain, and she constantly assessed her surroundings for threats.

For children who have experienced trauma, I always recommend work with a counselor. Many parents think a problem will resolve or get better on its own. They might ignore it, afraid that addressing the problem, or getting help for it, will make it more "real" in some way. But as you've probably found, this doesn't tend to work when it comes to trauma. Usually, if you or your kids are struggling with an issue, it will continue to be a struggle until you do something proactive to help deal with the problem. We don't just grow out of trauma. Therefore, it's important to be intentional and proactive about your child's healing, especially if they have experienced trauma in their past. This includes being proactive about getting your child professional help if needed.

VICARIOUS TRAUMA

Our children's experience of trauma doesn't just affect them—it can affect parents and all those who love and care for children as well. At the beginning of this chapter, I shared how engaging with children's experiences of trauma was one of the most difficult parts of my job as a therapist. The experience of opening ourselves up to a child who has been hurt and providing a container to hold their pain and suffering as they work through it is immensely powerful, but it can affect us in significant ways. It is critical to be aware of the effects of vicarious trauma so we can be vigilant in getting the support and help that we need as we support and help our kids.

In her book *Trauma Stewardship: An Everyday Guide to Caring for Self while Caring for Others*, Laura van Dernoot Lipsky lays out sixteen signs that a person may be dealing with vicarious trauma.[10] As you read through the signs, think about whether you have faced any of these symptoms as you help hold trauma that your child has experienced:

- Feeling helpless or hopeless
- Having a sense that you can never do enough, or that you should be doing more
- Hypervigilance
- Diminished creativity
- Inability to embrace complexity
- Minimizing
- Chronic exhaustion and physical ailments
- Inability to listen, or deliberate avoidance
- Dissociative episodes
- A sense of being persecuted
- Guilt
- Fear
- Anger and cynicism
- Inability to empathize, or numbing
- Addiction
- Intrusive images or stories

If you notice yourself experiencing vicarious trauma, be kind and compassionate with yourself. Helping another person work through trauma is difficult, especially when that person is a child you love. It's also critical to get the help and support you need. Trauma—even when it belongs to someone else—is a lot to carry. Who is supporting you in this journey? Who is a safe person you can talk to? I speak with adoptive and foster parents who often feel totally alone and that no one understands their situation. In fact, that is why I started Replanted: to help support adoptive and foster families so they wouldn't feel so alone.

In our first book, *Replanted: Faith-Based Support for Adoptive and Foster Families*,[11] we talk about three critical aspects of support: emotional, informational, and tangible. When it comes to dealing with vicarious trauma, emotional support is critical. Adoptive and foster parents are often so focused on giving, on meeting the needs of their children, that they forget it is also necessary to receive, to have their own needs met. It's not selfish to get the help and support you need. Just as our children need space and support to work through experiences of trauma, we need space and support to help us cope with the impact of our children's trauma on us. Getting your own help and support will help you be a better parent to your child.

DISCUSSION QUESTIONS

- What was your main takeaway as you read this chapter? What did you learn about trauma that you didn't know previously?
- How might understanding trauma give you a greater degree of empathy and understanding for your kids? How might it improve your relationship with them?
- What came up for you when you read the section on vicarious trauma? How has parenting a child affected by trauma affected you? How would you rate your level of help and support? How could you intentionally seek out additional support?

6

ATTACHMENT

One of the most important tasks that children undertake while growing up is to develop a secure attachment—a trusting bond or relationship—with their primary caregivers. When children experience the security of their parents or caregivers consistently meeting their needs over time, they feel safe to explore the world around them, knowing they can always come back to receive comfort if they get hurt or need assistance. This back-and-forth of going out into the world and coming back for support and help is indicative of secure attachment and a close bond between parent and child. This is what we hope for as parents—a child who can be independent and self-sufficient yet also connected and able to sustain deep relationships with others. Attachment is the building block of that process. As we grow, our attachment as a child provides the foundation for our relationships with others as an adult.

Unfortunately, building a secure attachment is often a challenge for adoptive and foster parents. Because of the disruption and trauma experienced by children who are adopted or in foster care, they often lack the trust necessary to build a secure attachment with their parents. Their early experiences have taught them that their needs may not be met, so they might be standoffish and keep you at arm's length. Or they might be clingy and reactive, always needing reassurance that you are there. Or they might not seek you for comfort when they get hurt, and may struggle to calm down when you offer it. Or they might respond seemingly at random, reacting one way today and a different way tomorrow. Children who have had multiple placements, have experienced severe neglect, or were raised in institutions with a high child-to-caregiver ratio are especially vulnerable to attachment difficulties because they never learned that an adult would take care of their needs. This can be true even for babies placed for adoption at birth. In utero, babies learned their mother's voice, the sound of her heartbeat, her smell, and more. Separation from this familiarity can affect a child's ability to attach to their adoptive parents. However your child responds, these behaviors can feel baffling and confusing. You long for your child to know they are safe and loved and that it is okay to connect with you. But for some reason, it continues to be a struggle.

Attachment theory can help us understand what is going on with our children, and in this chapter, we take a deep dive into attachment. What is attachment? How does it develop? What does it look like when it is going well, and what does it look like when it isn't?

TREY

Trey was a seven-year-old boy whom I worked with in counseling for over a year. I also counseled his foster parents, who eventually adopted him. As I learned more about Trey's history and experiences, I started to recognize that he had been through many challenging events that are risk factors for struggling with attachment.

Trey's biological parents were addicted to drugs and were an inconsistent presence in his life. When the Department of

Child and Family Services got involved and removed Trey from his home, he was placed with his aunt, along with his three siblings. Unfortunately, this kinship placement did not last very long. Trey's aunt had three children of her own, and she quickly became overwhelmed. After a few months, Trey was back in the system again. He was then placed in a foster home with his younger brother. Trey's two other siblings were placed in another foster home.

Trey wanted to go home and be with his mom, dad, and siblings. Unfortunately, Trey's parents were struggling to stop using drugs, and it didn't look like Trey would be returning home anytime soon. His mom missed visits frequently. Trey would get excited as a visit approached, and when it arrived, he often ended up waiting a long time for his mom to show up, only to be disappointed when she missed her visit again.

Not surprisingly, Trey had issues with abandonment. He was upset that he couldn't go home to be with his parents, and he felt abandoned by them. He also felt abandoned by his aunt. Even though living with her meant he wasn't living with his parents, he at least still got to live with all his siblings. Now his two older siblings were living in a different home, and he rarely saw them. Trey also showed some of these abandonment issues in his relationship with me. It was difficult for him to say goodbye at the end of each counseling session. We put goodbye rituals in place, and Trey needed to be reminded over and over that he would be able to see me again.

Trey struggled to adjust to his new foster home. Sometimes he tried to run away, and his foster parents would have to run after him and carry him back to the house. He also ran away from school, which caused bigger issues. Other times he got aggressive and acted out toward his foster parents and siblings. Trey's foster parents tried to support him and empathize with him, but they were getting worn out. It seemed hopeless that Trey would ever attach to them and trust them.

Like many kids who are adopted or in foster care, Trey had difficulty attaching to others. And it's easy to understand why: the people who were supposed to provide for him—his birth parents—weren't able to. Instead, they were inconsistent in meeting his needs, both physically and emotionally. Sometimes they were even physically and emotionally abusive. When children experience these kinds of things, it becomes difficult for them to form close relationships and trust people moving forward. Our relationships with our primary caregivers are a template for how we view relationships in the future. If our early relational experiences are negative, this shapes us to have negative expectations for future relationships.

Trey exhibited what we call disorganized attachment—his attachment behaviors didn't follow a coherent strategy. Sometimes he withdrew and ran away, whereas other times he desired comfort but acted out aggressively. It was hard to understand or predict what he would do—and his behaviors certainly were not adaptive in helping him get the love and support he needed.

ATTACHMENT 101

Research on attachment began in the mid-twentieth century. One of the first major research programs that had implications for child-parent attachment actually involved monkeys. Psychologist Harry Harlow conducted a series of now-infamous studies where he took young rhesus monkeys away from their mothers and provided them a choice between two "alternate" mothers.[1] One was made of wire but had a baby bottle of food, whereas the other was made of soft cloth but had no food. Interestingly, when the researchers looked at the amount of time spent between the two "mothers," monkeys did visit the wire "mother" to get food, but spent most of their time with the cloth "mother." The comfort (i.e., softness of the fabric) provided by the cloth mother seemed to be important for monkeys, and they would also turn to the cloth mother for comfort and security—going to the cloth mother for an embrace. This was the first breakthrough in understanding that comfort and nurture are important parts of development—it is not just about who provides the food.

Also in the twentieth century, researchers John Bowlby and Mary Ainsworth developed and fleshed out what we now call attachment theory. Bowlby was a child psychiatrist whose research linked child maladjustment with maternal deprivation and separation.[2] Bowlby eventually developed attachment theory, which focused on the early bonds formed by children and caregivers.[3] In contrast to behavioral psychologists who focused on food and sustenance as leading to attachment behavior, Bowlby focused on the process of nurturing and responding to the child's emotional needs.

Mary Ainsworth worked with Bowlby and extended his work on attachment. She is probably most famous for an experiment she created called the "strange situation test."[4] In this experiment, a child is placed into a room with their parent, and they explore the room and play together. Then a stranger enters the room and sits in a chair near the family. Then the parent leaves the room. Children would exhibit various responses when their parent left the room and they were left with a stranger: some children became visibly upset, while other children seemed unfazed. The final part of the test involves the parent returning to the room and trying to comfort the child. Researchers watched how a child responded when their parent left them with a stranger, but more importantly, they observed how the child responded when their parent returned. Was the child comforted by their parent? Did the child seek their parent out? Did the child ignore their parent? Using her observations of the child's response, as well as the child's interaction with their parent, Ainsworth identified three categories of attachment: (1) secure, (2) anxious or ambivalent, and (3) avoidant.

Describing how children from the three categories of attachment respond to the strange situation test paints a picture of each category. Secure children are able to explore their environment confidently when the parent is in the room—they use the parent as a "secure base" from which to explore. They also turn to the parent as a "safe haven" when they are feeling frightened and distressed. Secure children are distressed when their parent leaves the room, but are calmed by the parent relatively quickly once the parent returns. Secure children usually have a history of their parents consistently meeting their needs, and they trust that their parents will continue to meet their needs moving forward.

Anxious or ambivalent children are very upset and distressed when their parent leaves the room. However, the key difference between them and secure children is their difficulty calming down or being comforted when the parent returns. This attachment style can develop when parents meet their child's needs inconsistently. Because consistency is lacking, children don't necessarily trust that their needs will be met. Anxious or ambivalent children are sometimes described as overly dependent and clingy—but attachment theory explains how this can be viewed as a strategy they use to make sure their needs will be met.

Avoidant children tend not to be very upset when their parent leaves the room, and don't seek out the parent for comfort when they return. They might have trouble making close bonds or connections with their parents; instead, they rely on themselves. This attachment style can develop if a parent has trouble responding sensitively to the needs of their child. The child learns not to count on close relationships and that they must get their needs met on their own.

Later, a fourth attachment style was discovered: disorganized attachment.[5] Disorganized attachment is important to understand because some studies have found higher rates of disorganized attachment in alternative care settings such as institutions and foster homes.[6] Children who exhibit disorganized attachment show a mix of attachment-related behaviors, such as avoidance and resistance. Unlike children who are secure, anxious or ambivalent, or avoidant, all of whose attachment behaviors are "organized" in the sense that they have a consistent strategy for trying to get their needs met, disorganized children don't have a consistent way of engaging their parents. Children who exhibit disorganized attachment behaviors may have had inconsistent caregivers, or perhaps even caregivers who exhibited behaviors that rejected or were frightening to their child.

REACTIVE ATTACHMENT DISORDER

In some cases, a child's attachment difficulties may be so severe that they qualify for a diagnosis of reactive attachment disorder.[7] Reactive attachment disorder has three primary characteristics, all of which must be present for a diagnosis to be made by a licensed psychologist. First, the child must exhibit a consistent pattern of inhibited, emotionally withdrawn behavior in response to attachment-related behaviors from adults, such as rarely or minimally seeking out or responding to comfort when distressed. Second, the child must exhibit social and emotional disturbance—such as minimal social/emotional responsiveness; limited positive affect; and episodes of irritability, sadness, or fear even during nonthreatening interactions with adult caregivers. Third, the child must have experienced a pattern of extreme insufficient care, including social neglect or deprivation from caregivers, repeated changes of primary caregivers, or rearing in unusual settings that limit opportunities to form attachments.

Reactive attachment disorder is relatively rare—it occurs in less than 10 percent of severely neglected children—and a diagnosis is usually made before age five. However, if your child is exhibiting symptoms of reactive attachment disorder, it's a good idea to get a psychological evaluation by a licensed psychologist and get into counseling with a trauma-informed therapist.

BUILDING A SECURE ATTACHMENT

Now that we understand the different types of attachment, how can we help a child build a more secure attachment, including children who have experienced trauma or neglect? First, building a secure attachment is a lengthy process. It can't be done quickly or easily. A child's earliest experiences with their caregivers form the template for their attachment relationships moving forward. Those early experiences aren't reformatted or rewritten quickly or easily, and children don't just grow out of it. As parents, we must understand and accept that helping our children build a secure attachment will require a lot of work over a long time, especially if they have experienced trauma or neglect from their primary caregivers—so give yourself and your child grace during this time.

The key to helping kids build a secure attachment is to *consistently meet your child's needs over the long haul.* Because attachment is all about feeling secure in relationships with one's primary caregivers and trusting deep down that they will be there for you and consistently meet your physical and emotional needs, trust is key. The goal is for this new experience of having one's needs met to become what your child eventually views as the norm—the goal is to change your child's template. Little by little, children develop a stronger sense of security in their relationship with you.

Again, this isn't a quick or easy process. Some adoptive or foster parents think that because their home is safe and they are now able to provide for their child's physical and emotional needs, the child should now be able to develop a secure attachment. But it's not that easy. A child's sense of security can't be flipped on like a light switch. The early template for attachment relationships runs deep, and it isn't easy to alter. For little babies who cried and cried and no one came, they learned they have to take care of their own needs—no adult is coming. Little by little, as you consistently provide for your child's needs, their attachment is likely to shift. But we are talking about small shifts over time. It's important to celebrate even small changes.

What does it mean to *meet your child's needs*? Physical needs are fairly straightforward and generally well understood by parents. But it is worth saying anyway: It is critical to provide your child with adequate shelter, nutritious food, water, and sleep. It is amazing how some children who exhibit emotional or behavioral problems improve when parents make it a priority to feed their children nutritious meals and snacks throughout the day, or make sure their kids go to bed early so they get nine to ten hours of sleep each night. Being "hangry" is a real thing! If a child is tired and needs a nap, it's unrealistic to expect good behavior during this time. Make sure you meet these basic physical needs for your children.

Emotional needs can be more complicated. The best model I have seen for building secure attachment through meeting your child's needs is called the Circle of Security, as described in the book *Raising a Secure Child: How Circle of Security Parenting Can Help You Nurture Your Child's Attachment, Emotional Resilience, and Freedom to Explore*, by Kent Hoffman, Glen Cooper, and Bert Powell. I encourage any parent interested in learning more about this topic to pick up their book.

Briefly, the model says children have two main sets of needs. The first set of needs involves supporting your child's exploration. This is the "secure base" function of attachment. Children need to know you are a secure base from which to venture out and explore the world. This is how children grow and learn: by exploring their environment. For example, if you are a parent of a little one, you have probably noticed they venture out to play with their toys but periodically run back to you for a hug, and then off they go again. The child is using you as a secure base. Children struggle to explore if they don't have that secure base to venture out from. Key behaviors that support a child's exploration include watching over them, delighting in them, helping them, and enjoying the world with them.

As children venture out and explore the world, painful things happen. They might fall and bump their head or scrape their knee. When these things happen, children need support. The second set of needs has to do with welcoming children as they come back to you. This is the "safe haven" function of attachment. Children need to know you are there to support them when they need it. Key behaviors that welcome a child's coming back to you include protecting them, comforting them, delighting in them, and helping organize their feelings. (Note that delighting in your child can help meet both sets of needs.)

A natural back-and-forth happens when children have a secure attachment with their primary caregivers. As this process happens again and again, the child learns two important things: First, they are competent to go out and explore their world (and they learn that this is a good thing, because the caregiver encourages it). Second, when they need help and support, the caregiver will be there. They are not on their own. They can depend on the caregiver when they need help. If this process is repeated over a long period of time, the child will begin to develop a more secure attachment. Attachment styles are not fixed. They can change over time for both children and parents.

When you think about the Circle of Security model of attachment parenting, which side of the circle does your child struggle with the most—going out to explore or coming in for support and comfort? Which side of the circle do you struggle with the most—meeting your child's need to go out to explore or come in for support or comfort?

CONNECTING OUR ATTACHMENT AND OUR CHILD'S ATTACHMENT

The other important variable when it comes to helping our children develop healthy attachment is *us*. What is your attachment style? As Karyn Purvis, who cofounded the Karyn Purvis Institute of Child Development at Texas Christian University, said during a training I took with her, "We can't bring our children to a place of healing if we don't know the way ourselves." If you struggle to attach to your child and meet their needs for independence and exploration or connection and comfort, I strongly recommend individual counseling. A trained therapist can help you uncover how your childhood experiences shaped your attachment tendencies so you can experience growth and healing in your relationships moving forward. It's never too late.

The question of which side of the circle you struggle with the most in supporting your child's needs is an important one to consider. As we discussed in chapter 3, none of us had perfect parents. Each of us struggled to get some of our needs met in one way or another. And we tend to either (a) use the same parenting strategies that our parents used, or (b) react to the parenting strategies our parents used by doing the opposite. Neither of these strategies is adaptive or helpful for our children.

When you think about the two main sets of emotional needs that we have as children—going out to explore and coming in for support and comfort—what needs (if any) did your parents do a good job of meeting? What needs (if any) did your parents struggle to meet? For example, did your parents have a hard time letting you explore because they were anxious that something bad might happen? Or if you came to them for comfort, did they tell you something like "It didn't hurt that bad, you'll be fine"?

My parents were farmers, and they did a better job of meeting my need to go and explore than they did of my need to come in for support and comfort. My husband Josh was the opposite—his parents were counselors and did a better job of meeting his need to come in for support and comfort than to go out to explore. This can affect our parenting, as we find ourselves either replicating patterns and behaviors we've had modeled for us or reacting against those patterns and behaviors and swinging in the opposite direction. So it's important to reflect. When your child expresses a need to be independent and go out and explore, what is your reaction? Do you cheer on your child and support their independence? Or does this make you uncomfortable? Do you get nervous and anxious, encouraging your child to stay put instead?

What about when your child is hurt or crying and expresses a need to come in for comfort and support? Do you welcome your child in, give them hugs and kisses, and help them organize their feelings? Or does this make you uncomfortable? Do you tell them to buck up, or that "boys (or girls) don't cry"?

DISCUSSION QUESTIONS

- What stood out to you most as you read this chapter? What did you learn about attachment that you didn't know previously?
- How might understanding attachment help you move forward in your relationship with your kids? What needs is your child expressing that might be challenging for you to meet?
- What was your attachment relationship like with your primary caregivers? Can you see any connections between your attachment growing up and your challenges in your own parenting journey?

7

SENSORY PROCESSING DIFFICULTIES

Have you ever spent time with a child who couldn't sit still, needed a lot of physical stimulation, or became very upset because of a minor physical irritant such as the ridges on the inside of their socks? Many studies have shown that trauma—including the kinds of trauma commonly experienced by kids in foster care and adoption—can affect the brain, including how we process information from our senses.[1] This can lead to sensory processing difficulties, which can look like withdrawal from being touched, or excessive jumping, swinging, and spinning. But for those of us who don't struggle with these kinds of challenges, or don't understand them, it can be easy to view sensory processing difficulties as something else, such as ADHD or defiance.

Here's a quick exercise to help us understand sensory processing challenges. Right where you are sitting, pause what you are doing and pay attention to what you notice with your senses. First, get in touch with your sense of hearing. Focus in on what sounds you hear in the room. Maybe you hear sounds you didn't notice before. For example, as I am writing this chapter, I hear the dishwasher going *woosh-woosh* in

the distance. I hear my husband walking around the house—
stomp-stomp, stomp-stomp. I hear my daughter from the baby
monitor rustling around in her crib as she takes her nap. These
are sounds that are happening in the environment, but I wasn't
consciously aware of them before I stopped what I was doing
and focused on my hearing. What about you? What sounds do
you notice in your environment right now?

Most of us are naturally able to filter out unimportant
sounds in our environment so we can focus on what we need
to do. My senses automatically regulate the *woosh-woosh* of
the dishwasher so I don't notice it when I am trying to focus
on my writing. But for some of our kids, their senses work
differently. They can't modulate sounds as easily, so they hear
the *woosh-woosh* of the dishwasher at the same level as your
instructions to them, for example. It's more difficult to operate
in the world when our senses aren't automatically adjusting
the levels of sounds in our environment.

Let's try it again, but instead of focusing on your sense
of hearing, focus on your sense of touch. You might not be
actively touching anything. But sit quietly, right where you are,
and see whether you can notice anything touching your body.
For example, when I paused my writing and focused on my
sense of touch, I noticed cool air blowing against my body
from the air conditioner vent on the ceiling. I also noticed the
tightness of my socks and shoes on my feet, and the weight
of a blanket and my laptop computer on my lap. What about
you? What things do you notice right now with your sense
of touch?

Again, most of us can modulate our sense of touch. For
example, I didn't notice the cool air blowing against my body
until I stopped and focused on it. Same with my socks and
shoes and the blanket on my lap. I mostly go through life not

being in tune with how my body is interacting with my environment through my sense of touch. But for some kids, this isn't the case. Some children are very sensitive to temperature, and the cool air blowing on their body could feel very uncomfortable. Other children might feel uncomfortable with the little seam that sticks out on the inside of their socks, or the tag on their shirt. Some children might hate to have a blanket on their lap; others might do well with a heavier blanket weighing them down. And this applies to all our senses. For a child with sensory processing challenges, it can be hard to organize all the inputs they receive. For me, it's easy to drown out all the sensory input I am receiving to continue writing. But for those with sensory challenges, it's hard to organize their environment. It's like everything is being played at the same volume.

ALEXANDER

Alexander was a six-year-old boy who was adopted internationally from Romania. He had a sensory processing difficulty we refer to as being *sensory overresponsive*, meaning he experienced sensory overload—stimuli from the environment were perceived as louder or more extreme than they would be by an average person. However, it took his parents awhile to figure out what was going on with Alexander. (This is fairly common. Sensory processing challenges aren't well understood, sometimes even by mental health professionals. Because of this, kids who struggle with sensory processing issues can often go undiagnosed or be misdiagnosed.)

The main problem that Alexander's parents noticed was that he would run away and hide in dark places, like his closet. There didn't seem to be an obvious trigger for his behavior, at least not that his parents noticed. It just seemed like Alexander would get upset suddenly and leave the room. This was particularly common when they were around big groups of people or in settings with a lot of noise or activity.

Eventually, Alexander's parents had him assessed by an occupational therapist. Occupational therapy is a branch of healthcare that helps people who have physical, sensory, or cognitive challenges, and specializes in assessing and helping with sensory processing disorders. This is where Alexander's parents learned that he was likely sensory overresponsive, meaning he was experiencing the stimuli in his environment at a higher "volume" than the average person.

Understanding what was going on with Alexander was helpful for his parents. For example, when Alexander ran away and hid in dark places, he wasn't trying to be defiant. He was trying to turn down (or turn off) the sensory input he was experiencing, which was uncomfortable and sometimes painful for him. In addition to increasing his parents' understanding of why Alexander was acting this way, the occupational therapist also suggested some relatively straightforward strategies to help Alexander cope with his sensory processing challenges. For example, Alexander's parents got him a pair of noise-canceling headphones to wear when noises in the environment were too loud and overwhelming. This gave him a helpful coping skill to moderate the stimuli in his environment. Alexander's parents knew it was important to remember his headphones whenever they went to loud events, like a high school football game.

They also brainstormed other strategies to help further regulate Alexander's environment. For example, they worked with Alexander to declutter his room so he was not as overwhelmed with all the things in his space. Alexander's parents were more mindful about the events they went to with Alexander. For example, they decided not to go out to the park and watch fireworks on the Fourth of July, because, with all the crowds and loud noises, they knew this would not be a pleasant experience for Alexander. These were simple shifts that they made in their family life that made a big difference for Alexander—and for them.

SENSORY PROCESSING DIFFICULTIES

What is the role of our senses, and what challenges can they present? Our senses take in information and stimuli from the environment, which is then processed in our central nervous system. When you were growing up, you probably learned about the five main senses: sight, smell, taste, hearing, and touch. There are two more senses you may not have learned about in school: vestibular (balance) and proprioception (sense of where you are in space). If your sensory system is working well, you may not even think about your senses or be aware of them (apart from enjoying a nice meal or the smell of roses). But children who have sensory processing difficulties struggle to process, organize, and interpret the sensory information they take in—something most of us do automatically—as they go about their day.

Children with sensory processing difficulties can exhibit behavioral, physical, and psychosocial symptoms.[2] Behavioral symptoms can include withdrawal from being touched, refusal to eat certain foods, hypersensitivity to fabrics or tags, dislike of hands being dirty, oversensitivity to odors or sounds, tendency to notice or hear background noises others can't, tendency to harm others accidently during physical play, and lack of engagement in creative play. Physical symptoms can include fatigue; excessive jumping, swinging, and spinning; poor coordination or balance; high pain tolerance; clumsiness; delayed gross or fine motor skills; and constant motion. Psychosocial symptoms can include standing too close to others, fear of crowds, fear of surprise touch, decreased ability to interact with peers, depression, and anxiety.

In her book *The Out-of-Sync Child: Recognizing and Coping with Sensory Processing Disorder*, teacher and author Carol Kranowitz discusses three main subtypes of sensory processing difficulties: (1) sensory modulation disorder, (2) sensory discrimination disorder, and (3) sensory-based motor disorder.[3] I briefly describe each subtype in the following paragraphs, but if you think your child has sensory processing challenges, it is critical to get an occupational therapy assessment. My hope is that these descriptions give you a general idea about common sensory processing difficulties, but it's always important to get a professional opinion.[4]

Sensory modulation disorder involves challenges regulating one's responses to sensory input.[5] Some kids, like Alexander in the previous section, might be overresponsive to sensory input, meaning they experience sensory overload. For example, they might avoid touching or being touched by others, or react in an extreme way to certain textures, noises, or smells. Other children might be underresponsive, meaning they react less strongly than usual to sensory input. For example, they might be unaware of being touched, respond slowly to things happening in their environment, or ignore ordinary sounds or voices. Still other kids might be sensory craving, meaning they seek out stimulation from their environment. For example, they might move constantly, fidget, like spinning around, or crave bear hugs.

The other two sensory processing difficulties are less common. Sensory discrimination disorder occurs when a child has trouble distinguishing one sensation from another or has difficulty understanding what a sensation means.[6] For example, they might have poor body awareness or ability to process pain and temperature, such as trouble knowing whether they are hot or cold. Or they might have difficulty hearing the differences between sounds, especially consonants at the end of words, such as differentiating "cap" from "cat."

Finally, sensory-based motor problems have two subtypes.[7] One subtype is postural disorder, which involves problems with movement, balance, and bilateral coordination. A child might have trouble maintaining their balance, or may have difficulty using both sides of the body together when doing things like jumping, clapping, or catching balls. The second subtype is dyspraxia, which means the child has trouble with coordinated and voluntary actions. They might have trouble performing actions that require multiple steps put together, like playing on playground equipment, writing, or using eating utensils.

HOW TO HELP

If you think your child has sensory processing difficulties, the most important step is to get an assessment with an occupational therapist. As noted earlier, sensory processing difficulties can be challenging to understand and are often misdiagnosed (even by mental health therapists). Instead of trying to diagnose your child yourself, it's critical for them to see a professional.

What should you consider when choosing an occupational therapist? Make sure the occupational therapist has experience assessing and treating children with sensory processing challenges. Before seeing an occupational therapist, check out their website or talk with them on the phone and ask them about the primary populations they serve, as well as their specialties. If you live in a rural area, you may not have much of a choice when it comes to occupational therapy, but if you live in a big city, you may find occupational therapists who specialize in treating children with sensory processing challenges.

What happens when you go in to see an occupational therapist for the first time? The occupational therapist will begin by giving your child a full assessment, which usually includes a battery of tests, as well as observations of your child and interviews with the child's caregivers. Based on this assessment, the occupational therapist will design a treatment plan to help your child better integrate their sensory experiences, often called sensory integration therapy. Examples of things the occupational therapist might have your child do are spinning and swinging using specialized equipment in a sensory gym, wearing weighted vests or entering a squeeze machine, or providing deep pressure. Because occupational therapists will likely see your child only one to two hours per week, they will also give you exercises you can practice with your child at home to continue the work they are doing in therapy.

Before the first appointment, be a detective and keep a journal of observations to discuss with the occupational therapist. Pay attention to what your child seeks out or avoids, and write those things down. See if you notice patterns in your child's environment that are related to meltdowns (is it loud? bright? do they frequently melt down when they are told they can't climb up the slide?). Gathering this information can be helpful to identify patterns or triggers for your child that an occupational therapist could address with specific intervention.

Is there anything you can do on your own besides taking your child to an occupational therapist? It's hard to give general suggestions because interventions will depend on your child and their issues. But it can be useful to think about your child's sensory needs and help them design coping skills to meet those needs.

For example, if your child appears to need higher levels of sensory input than normal (sensory underresponsive), it might be that encouraging your child to "calm down" and take deep breaths won't be effective, because your child actually needs the opposite (higher levels of sensory stimulation). Instead, to help regulate their feelings, encourage your child to jump up and down on a trampoline or do wall pushes. On the other hand, if your child appears to need lower levels of sensory input than normal (sensory overresponsive), another strategy is likely needed. Buying your child noise-canceling headphones or providing them a quiet, calm space might be important.

DISCUSSION QUESTIONS

- What stood out to you most as you read this chapter? What did you learn about sensory processing difficulties that you didn't know previously?
- How does your child take in sensory input? Have you noticed any difficulties or challenges? Using the three sensory processing difficulties we discussed in this chapter, how would you categorize the challenges?
- What do you think about getting your child an assessment with an occupational therapist? What questions or concerns do you have about this process?

8

CULTURAL AND SOCIAL ADJUSTMENT

Our culture permeates almost every aspect of our lives, including family, religion, and political views, but we aren't always aware of the ways it shapes our experience of the world and of each other. Before we get too far into discussing culture and how it can influence adoptive and foster parenting, it's important to define what exactly we are talking about. Culture is a broad term that refers to how our social upbringing and the different groups we are a part of help define our norms and expectations for the world. Our cultural worldview can have a huge impact on our beliefs, values, attitudes, and relationships. Our cultural background and worldview can influence every aspect of our life, from where we choose to live, to what kind of education we get, to what kind of work we do, to whether we believe in God and go to church, to whom we choose to marry.

What contributes to our cultural worldview? Our cultural worldview is received from others who are important to us. For example, our family of origin has a strong influence on what we believe and how we see the world. We receive inputs to our cultural worldview from other sources as well, such as the country and geographic location where we grew up and the groups in the community we are involved with—religious institutions, schools, and cultural groups. Different aspects of our identity, such as race and ethnicity, gender, sexual orientation, and socioeconomic status, might shape our cultural worldview as we engage with others and are treated in certain ways because of those identities. We take these various cultural inputs and internalize them, creating a unique way of seeing the world.

What about you? When you think about your cultural worldview, what are some of the strongest factors that influence how you see the world? If you are having trouble thinking about this issue, one place to start might be your religious upbringing. How did religion and your faith community shape your view of the world?

When you have a biological child, that child is socialized into your family culture from the beginning. Also, a biological child most likely shares most cultural identities with you, or if not you, then their other parent. There are some exceptions, of course—for example, you might be straight and your child might be gay. But because of the influence of genetics, most cultural identities will be shared. This makes some aspects of parenting easier—for example, a Black parent can more easily help their Black child develop a positive racial and ethnic identity because the parent went through this process themselves and knows its importance. They are also likely connected to a community of people who share their race and ethnicity, and are better connected to role models and mentors who are people of color.

These issues can be challenging for adoptive or foster parents who have a child from a different cultural background. This can range from visible differences in immutable categories such as race and ethnicity to more fluid categories like beliefs, values, and attitudes shaped by the cultural groups they have spent time in. It can feel difficult to bridge the gap. How can parents welcome a child into their family (which has an established and shared cultural worldview) while also working to honor the child's cultural background and perspective?

JENNIFER

I met Jennifer when she was in her mid-twenties. She was working an entry-level job in an insurance company, her first job after graduating from college. Jennifer, who is Black, had been adopted as a baby, and her adoptive parents, who were White, had also adopted her younger brother. Eventually, our conversation got around to what it was like growing up in her adoptive family. Jennifer had a lot of interesting things to say about what it was like to grow up as a Black girl in a White family.

Jennifer said that growing up, she didn't think much about being Black or her racial identity. She was just trying to fit in, and fitting in meant trying to be like her family and community, which was mostly White. Her parents and siblings were all White, except for her younger biological brother, who was also Black. They lived in a predominantly White neighborhood in a predominantly White town and attended a predominantly White church. Jennifer's parents didn't talk much about her being Black—Jennifer said they didn't know what to say or how to address it. It just wasn't much of a focus. Sometimes she would notice she was treated differently by others, and it did bring up some questions. Was it because she was Black? Was it because she was adopted? As she got older, she could see people trying to piece together their family story when she called a White woman "Mom."

It wasn't until Jennifer went to college and moved to a larger nearby city that she realized something was missing in her development, and it had to do with race. For the first time, Jennifer was living in a diverse community and meeting other Black friends. She realized she didn't know much about her own culture. Where did she fit in? She didn't fully connect with her family's White culture. And she didn't fully connect with her Black culture. But both were part of her. It felt uncomfortable, and Jennifer had to do a lot of exploring of her racial identity on her own as an adult.

She began to question some of the decisions her parents made. At first, it seemed good that she was treated just like everyone else in her family—but she began to realize her experience as a Black woman *was* different, and her family not acknowledging that felt painful. The only connections her parents had to Black people were to her and her brother. What did it mean that they kept their distance from Black people and the Black community? Did her parents feel threatened, uncomfortable, or disengaged? What did that mean for their relationship with her?

By the time I met her, Jennifer had grown more comfortable with her racial identity and was attending a multiracial church. She looked around at her diverse city and community and wondered, "Why didn't my parents choose to live here when I was growing up?" Race had been an uncomfortable topic for Jennifer then. Either it wasn't talked about or it was addressed in a way that felt forced. She understood now that her race was a big part of who she was and how other people viewed her. Her parents tried their best, but looking back, she wished they would have done more to help her navigate her racial identity, or at least connected her with other folks who could help.

THE IMPORTANCE OF CULTURE

The first thing to keep in mind when thinking about adopting or fostering a child from a different cultural background is that their cultural identity is important—it has to be recognized, honored, and nurtured. It is going to be a big part of our children's lives, and if we want to love and parent them well, it must be a big part of our lives as well. I would even be so bold to say that if you are not willing to fully submerge your family life into your child's culture of origin, you should think critically about whether you should adopt a child from a different race or culture. Children are observant. If you say "I love everything about you" to your child who is Korean but you have no Korean friends, that can speak volumes about what you think about a huge part of your child's identity.

Some of us—especially those of us from dominant cultures—don't like to talk about culture and cultural differences, because it can be uncomfortable. So many of the issues at the heart of our current polarization—like protests over systemic racism, undocumented immigration, LGBTQ rights, and gender roles—are deeply rooted in culture. Sometimes we hope that by avoiding talking about these issues, we can avoid conflict. Part of this avoidance may have to do with privilege—discussions about culture and cultural differences can remind us of the privilege we have.

If we are parenting a child from a different cultural background, we might also worry that because they are experiencing a lot of transition already, it would be too much to focus on how they are different from us. We are trying to help them fit in to our family, and it might be easier if everyone focused on what we have in common, rather than our differences. So we might minimize (perhaps unconsciously) our child's cultural differences.

But our child will have to navigate the world around them. They bring with them their cultural identities that shape how other people view them and how they view themselves. These identities aren't something we can (or want to) forget or put into a closet. They help make us who we are. Children who are adopted or spend time in foster care grow up missing a piece of their development when their parents ignore their cultural identities. Later in life, they may feel frustrated or resentful about this as they begin to explore what it means to have a cultural identity of their own. Thus, as adoptive and foster parents, we need to help our children engage and explore their cultural identities (to the extent they want to) from an early age.

CULTURAL HUMILITY

Before we get into the nuts and bolts of engaging our children's cultural backgrounds, I'd like to look at the attitudes we bring to the idea of cultural differences. When engaging with cultural differences, it can be easy to think about our own cultural background and perspective as better than someone else's. We typically wouldn't admit to it or even realize it's true of us, but this is a pretty normal thing. Your cultural worldview has worked well for you. It has helped you define what is important to you and to live a life that aligns with your values. It was shaped by your environment growing up, and is often supported by others who view the world in a similar way. You might have friends who think similarly, or maybe you are a part of a close-knit community, like a church whose members share a similar cultural worldview. Most people see their own cultural perspective as the "right" way to view the world—it's just how you do things.

It can be easy to look down on others who have a different perspective and judge them as wrong, misguided, or perhaps even evil. Their cultural worldview and perspective may not make sense to you at all. You likely have some areas of bias—or preference—toward certain cultural groups. We all have biases. It's part of growing up in a society that judges certain cultural perspectives as good and others as bad.

For example, in the news this week, a video emerged of two teens fighting in a mall—one was White and one was Black. The video caught a lot of attention because of racial profiling by the police officers. In the video, you see the officers intervene. The officer that grabs the White boy pulls him to the side and sits him down on a couch. The other officer pins the Black teen to the ground aggressively. Both officers then restrain the Black teen and handcuff him while the White boy sits (unaccompanied by an officer) on the couch. Why is this? Both teens were fighting and were equally a threat, but the two teens are treated differently. This is a prime example of racial prejudice—seeing the Black teen as a threat and the White teen as not a threat. (If you're interested and open to considering areas where you might have bias, go online and take the Implicit Association Test.[1] This quick test can identify the extent of your unconscious associations linking certain groups with positive words and other groups with negative words.)

You may also rely on stereotypes when thinking about other cultural groups—some you may realize and others you may not. A stereotype is a shortcut that involves a generalized belief about a particular group of people. Stereotypes help us organize a great deal of information quickly. We may not have the time to get to know every person individually, so it saves cognitive time and energy if we can rely on a shortcut. The problem, however, is that stereotypes put people in a box in an unfair way—limiting their opportunities to express who they really are.

So what might be a more helpful perspective or attitude for engaging cultural differences? One framework I have found helpful is cultural humility.[2] To begin, we acknowledge we all have a certain lens through which we view the world, and that lens is shaped by our own cultural background and experiences. We have found a way of viewing the world that works for us, but it isn't the only way to view the world. We can then see that others may have a different cultural perspective—and that's okay. Once we acknowledge that, we can take this awareness into relationship by being open to another person's cultural point of view. This is particularly important when we are parenting a child from a different cultural background, because cultural humility allows us to honor and respect our child's cultural background and worldview rather than expecting the child to conform to our family's cultural norms and expectations.

HONORING YOUR CHILD'S CULTURAL BACKGROUND

Now that we have considered some unhelpful and helpful attitudes that we often bring to culture and cultural differences, let's focus on practicalities. How can we as parents honor our child's cultural background? What can we do to help our kids engage their cultural background and develop their cultural identity? In this section, we will primarily explore issues around race and ethnicity, but other cultural identities, such as sexual orientation, religion, and socioeconomic status, can also apply.

Think about your environment

One recommendation I hear a lot when talking with transracial families is the importance of living in diverse spaces. In the United States and Canada, most transracial adoptions involve families where one or both parents are White.[3] Many of us live, work, go to school, and attend church in settings where most people look like us, perhaps in part because it feels more comfortable. But if you adopt or foster a child from a different cultural background, think critically about the diversity of the spaces where you spend your time. It is helpful if kids are in environments where families and kids look like them because they can have role models and peers who share their cultural identities. Over and over again I hear from kids who grew up in a transracial family how difficult it was to be the only kid who looked like them in their family, school, and faith community.

If you are serious about providing your child with a supportive environment culturally, you must take active steps into spaces that are more culturally comfortable for your child. I have talked with families who have changed jobs and moved to a different city because the setting they were living in was almost one hundred percent White. But even if you can't pick up and move to another city, you may have options about what neighborhood to live in, what school your children will attend, and what church you go to as a family. If you are White, intentionally choose settings that are more diverse, places where your child will interact regularly with people who look like them. Note that engaging in more diverse spaces may take you out of your comfort zone. However, this is likely only a small piece of what your child is feeling when they navigate all-White spaces. Also, think about the messages we might be sending to our child if we refuse to engage in culturally diverse spaces. We don't want to send our child the message that (except for them) we prefer to be in the company of White people.

Mentors and role models

Our environment also shapes the mentors and role models available to our children. For children of color in communities where most people do not look like them, having mentors and role models who share their racial and cultural background is particularly important. These individuals can provide them an example or template for what is possible. Plus, they can give your child a safe place to process a huge piece of their identity. This is part of the reason why representation in broader culture is so important. As I am writing this book, for example, the current vice president of the United States is a woman of color. Before Kamala Harris, a woman, let alone a woman of color, had never served as vice president. Sure, you can tell girls they can do anything, but it often doesn't feel possible until you see it happen. Now my daughter will grow up knowing firsthand that a woman can serve as vice president, and that could very well change the way she thinks about her own future.

It is important to proactively work to connect your child with mentors or role models who share their race and ethnicity. If you are making sure your environment is diverse, this should hopefully happen naturally, because you will be developing real relationships with other adults in the community who share your child's race and ethnicity. Connecting your child with a teacher, pastor, or coach who shares the child's race and ethnicity can help develop their racial and ethnic identity in a way that you cannot if you don't share your child's race and ethnicity.

Learn with your child

It can also be helpful to offer opportunities for your child to learn about their cultural background. Some examples of learning opportunities include museums, books, documentaries, cultural events, cultural camps, cooking food, speaking or learning the child's native language, or travel to the child's country of origin. Importantly, however, this process will be more effective if you are actively engaged in learning with your child. You need to have genuine interest and excitement for learning about your child's cultural background. If you don't care about the cultural learning, the experience may fall flat. By joining with your child in learning about their cultural background, you will communicate to them that their culture is important to you and worthy of investment.

Similarly, it's important that parents are open with their children about areas where they may have fallen short. I've worked with many children who felt hurt by their parents' lack of acknowledgment or learning about their child's culture of origin, and instead of listening to their child's feedback, they got defensive. This will only harm your relationship with your child. Hear your child out and explore the pain they may feel around this. Is there any truth to what they are sharing? What can you own and take responsibility for?

Initiate conversation, but respect where your child is at
Something I have learned about kids who have been trans-racially adopted is that their interest in their cultural background and identities shifts and changes over the years. In some phases of life, kids may not seem to care about their cultural background at all. They just aren't engaged in it—they might be more focused on things like making the basketball team or trying to find a date for the prom. At other times, their cultural identity may be very important for how they are doing and what they are focused on.

As parents, it's important to initiate conversation and learning with your child about their cultural background and identities, but it's also important to respect where your child is at the moment. If your child doesn't want to talk about their cultural background or engage in a learning opportunity, don't force it. Get comfortable with offering opportunities, but ultimately let your child decide when or how to engage. Their level of engagement may increase or decrease over time, and that's okay. Your job is to provide the opportunity for conversation and engagement, but you don't have to make it happen.

This is another reason to live in diverse spaces and have mentors and role models for your children: If diversity is part of your environment and you and your children have relationships with people who share their cultural background, this conversation and engagement can happen more naturally. It's part of the world you live in, rather than something extra you are trying to get your child to do.

FAMILY SYSTEMS AND TRADITIONS

Much of this chapter has focused on broader cultural identities, like race and ethnicity, nationality, religion, gender, and sexual orientation. But it's also important to consider that your family has its own culture of sorts, and your new child may be coming from a family that does things quite differently. There's a big adjustment when children join a new family.

As parents, how can we welcome our child into our family system and soften the transition that will occur? Again, cultural humility is key. Can you ask about what your child is used to and perhaps incorporate some of your child's traditions and interests or even create new traditions together? This can be easier said than done, but it's important. I remember a teenager sharing that on Christmas morning, his biological family would wake up early and tear into all their presents before breakfast. He loved that tradition. But at his new foster home, the family went to church in the morning and then opened presents one at a time after dinner. He missed his Christmas tradition.

When we adopt or foster a child, we often expect the child will come into our house and join in our traditions and do things the way we have always done them. It's as if we are standing across the room from our child and we expect them to come all the way over to our side. Our arms are open, so it feels to us like we're welcoming them in. But we're still asking them to meet us on our terms. It's impossible to completely change your family system and traditions, but could you meet your child halfway? Might there be a way to change your family system to incorporate your child's traditions and interests?

DISCUSSION QUESTIONS

- What stood out to you most as you read this chapter? What did you learn about culture that you didn't know previously?

- What is most challenging for you when engaging with your child around their cultural background? What is most difficult about navigating cultural differences?

- What are some practical ways to honor, respect, and engage with your child around their cultural background and identities?

9

GRIEF AND LOSS

For most adoptive and foster parents, welcoming a new child into the home is a time of joyful celebration. What can get lost is how this process often carries with it a great deal of grief and loss for our children. It's difficult to hold the tension between these contrasting sets of feelings existing in the same reality. When parents have prayed and worked hard and waited so long to prepare their hearts and homes for the arrival of a new child, it can be tough to know how to engage children who are experiencing this moment very differently— or to realize they may be having a different experience entirely.

Before we get too far into the content of this chapter, I invite you to think back to a time when you experienced a significant loss. Go back to that place in your mind. What was it like to go through that loss? What was your experience of grief like? How did you react emotionally, physically, relationally, and spiritually?

As you remember what it was like to be in that place, think about how the people closest to you reacted to your grief and loss. What did they do? What did they say? What responses from others were helpful? What responses from others were less helpful? What did you need most from others during your time of grief and loss?

To begin thinking about how to engage our children around their experiences of grief and loss, it can be helpful to go back to our own experiences. It can give us empathy for what our kids are going through, and it can also give us some clues about what our children need most in their own experience. Many of us struggle to engage others' grief and loss in a helpful way. We might try to give advice, to minimize the pain, to look for the light at the end of the tunnel, or to make them feel better. Most of these "fix it" strategies aren't very effective, and they aren't honoring or respectful of the loss itself.

Working with grief and loss has a deep spiritual component as well. How can we join in God's work as we comfort those who mourn? How can we be the hands and feet of Jesus as we walk with our kids in their experience of deep sadness about the loss or rupture of their birth family? These are difficult questions, and there are no easy answers. Every single child who has experienced adoption or foster care has experienced grief and loss. It may manifest in different ways, and a child may not yet be able to verbalize it that way, but the loss is there. In this chapter, we will discuss some strategies to engage with our child's grief process in a more helpful way.

THE JOHNSON FAMILY

I met the Johnson family while counseling their son Brandon. Brandon was five years old and had been in foster care for almost a year before he was adopted by the Johnsons. The Johnsons were understandably happy and excited—they had struggled with infertility before becoming foster parents, and they loved Brandon so much. They felt called by God to help provide a family and safe home to children in need, and they were excited to build their family through adoption.

Brandon was excited, too, but he had a mix of emotions. He was old enough to know that being adopted by the Johnsons meant he would never go back to his birth family. He loved his birth mother and was sad and confused about why she wouldn't do the things she needed to do to get him back. He sometimes said things like "Why can't I go back to my birth family? Does my birth mom not want me?"

On his adoption day, the Johnsons were so happy. They posted pictures of their family posing with the judge with a caption that said, "I spent 282 days in foster care and now I'm adopted!" Friends and family members were congratulating the Johnsons and Brandon specifically, saying how excited they were that the adoption had gone through. Lots of likes and heart emojis were given.

I saw the excitement and the social media posts, and I felt sad. Was it wrong to be happy and excited about the adoption? No—all feelings are okay, and there is a lot to celebrate about adoption and the start of a new family. The key, however, is making sure we are creating space for all the feelings our children may have, including emotions that may be uncomfortable, such as grief and loss.

You might have seen adoption videos on social media where a family makes a surprise announcement to their child that they are being adopted. Often the child bursts into tears. Most of us probably assume we're looking at happy tears (perhaps thinking, "What a sweet moment for this family, that this child gets to be theirs forever!"). And maybe they truly are happy tears. But maybe, just maybe, they are more. Maybe the tears are from being overwhelmed by everything they have just learned. Maybe they are sad tears that come from the realization they will never return to their birth family. Our kids might not be feeling the same way we are. And even if they are, they are still experiencing loss.

When the Johnsons expressed so much happiness and excitement, it was hard for Brandon to share he was also feeling sad about the adoption and the realization that he would never go home to be with his birth mother. These were valid emotions that Brandon needed to work through, but he felt bad and pushed them down because he also loved his new family and didn't want to rain on their parade.

LOSS IN ADOPTION AND FOSTER CARE

Those of us who haven't experienced it firsthand can struggle to understand the grief and loss experienced by many children who are adopted or in foster care. Here are a few of the most common losses:

- *Loss of one's birth parents.* Even if a child was hurt by their birth parents or had a very challenging time with their birth family, many still feel a significant loss if the decision is made to establish permanence with a different family. Most of us long to be loved and accepted by our birth family, and it's painful when that family is broken.

- *Loss of one's birth siblings.* As much as foster care agencies try to keep siblings together, this is not always possible, and many children in foster care get separated from their siblings. Children may also have full or half-siblings they do not know about because of separation from their birth family, and wondering whether they have siblings out there is its own kind of grief.

- *Loss of one's extended family.* Many children are connected not only with their immediate birth family but also with their extended family. Some families are very integrated with grandparents, aunts and uncles, and cousins. A permanent placement can mean these relationships are lost. Even if they are not lost, they are usually changed.

- *Loss of temporary caregivers.* Some children end up in multiple foster homes for various reasons. Some children are relinquished. Some children are reunited with their birth families through foster care. Saying goodbye to foster parents and other temporary caregivers can be a huge loss for a child that formed a loving attachment with them.

- *Loss of knowing where one came from.* Many of us long to understand where we came from and why we are the way we are. When children are separated from their birth families, they lose this important link to the past and their history.

- *Loss of cultural and racial identity.* In the previous chapter, we talked about the importance of helping our children stay connected with their culture. But no matter what, a loss occurs when a child is removed from their birth parents or culture and is placed with a family that does not share their cultural or racial background. The child often misses something by not growing up around their culture, even if adoptive and foster parents do their best to help.

- *Loss of culture of origin.* For children who have been adopted internationally, they also lose experiences and knowledge around their country of origin.

- *Loss of control.* We all like to be in control and direct our own lives. This is true of both children and adults. When a child is adopted or placed in foster care, they lose control of one of the most important aspects of life—where we will live. Even if a child wants to stay with their birth family, this decision is not up to them.

- *Loss of belonging.* One of our core needs is to feel that we belong. We aren't meant to do life alone, and we do better if we feel that we are accepted by a group and by society at large. The first place of belonging is the family. When children have to leave their birth family, they are often leaving the place where they first felt that they belonged. And when they are a placed with a new family, they may or may not feel that they fit in.

- *Loss of answers to questions.* Children who are adopted or in foster care often have many questions about themselves and their upbringing. For example, children may not have photos of themselves as a baby, may not know their medical record, or may not know their actual birthday. They may wonder, Do I look like my mom? Do I like soccer because my dad liked soccer? If my parents saw me, would they feel proud of me? Why didn't my mom get me back? Why didn't my dad love me enough to get sober? Many of these questions don't have easy answers, and some are impossible to answer.

HELPING CHILDREN NAVIGATE GRIEF AND LOSS

What can we do as parents to help our children navigate their losses and cope with their feelings? How can we help them incorporate grief and loss into their lives in a healthy way? Here are some key things to remember.

Be okay with grief and loss

Grief and loss are a normal and healthy part of life. Life has many ups and downs. When you live a full life, you will love people who pass away. Sometimes accidents or tragedies happen that are beyond your control. Even if your life is going exactly as you would like, you will still experience grief and loss. There isn't a way to get away from it. It is part of how the world works and part of what it means to be a human being.

When we engage with our children, however, we may want to try to take away their grief and loss. We wish it weren't there, so we try to minimize or even reject it. Or we focus on the positive and try to redirect any feelings of grief and loss. This behavior often says more about our anxiety and discomfort than it does about our care for our child. We can't take away our children's experiences of loss or their feelings of grief. So we shouldn't try. Their experiences and feelings are valid, and we need to be okay with that. If your child experiences grief and loss, it doesn't mean you are a bad parent or that they don't love or appreciate you. It simply means your child is experiencing a normal emotion that almost always makes sense given what they have been through.

Offer your presence

When a child is experiencing grief and loss, the most important thing you can offer them is your presence. Sometimes parents feel that they must "do something" or "say the right thing." This often relates to our need to do something to "fix" a child's experience. There usually isn't one right thing to do or say when a child is struggling with grief and loss. Instead of worrying about what to say or do, just be with your child. Spend time with your child. Listen to them and ask them questions about their experience. Empathize with their feelings and validate their experience. For example, "I imagine you are feeling sad that you can no longer live with your birth mother. It's okay to feel sad about that. I would feel that way too."

If appropriate for your child, offer reassuring physical touch (hold them, give them hugs, etc.). Let them know you are there for them, and that you will continue to be there for them no matter what.

Grief is a process

In 1969, Swiss-American psychiatrist Elisabeth Kübler-Ross introduced a model for understanding grief that still shapes our understanding of the process we all must go through.[1] Based on her work with terminally ill patients, she noted five steps or stages of grief: (1) denial, (2) anger, (3) bargaining, (4) depression, and (5) acceptance. In the first stage, denial, a person might deny that the loss happened, or might live in an alternate reality. For example, a child might still believe they are going home to be with their birth parents, even though the parents' rights have been terminated. In the second stage, anger, a person might become frustrated and angry about the loss. A child might rage, throw a temper tantrum, or break something. In the third stage, bargaining, a person might believe they can change or avoid the loss through negotiation. A child might think, "If I'm really good and behave, then I will go back to my birth parents." In the fourth stage, depression, a person might feel down and depressed when the reality and finality of the loss sets in. A child might withdraw from normal activities and connections, feel numb, not want to get out of bed, or even have suicidal thoughts. In the final stage, acceptance, a person's emotions begin to stabilize and they return to baseline. They are not necessarily okay with the loss, but they believe that they will be okay.

There has been some criticism of the Kübler-Ross model, and much of this critique has focused on the idea that the process of grief is linear. Some people may not experience all the stages, and others may not experience the stages in the same order. (More recently, some have suggested that the stages of grief are better conceptualized as *states* of grief.[2]) This is important to understand when helping a child work through grief and loss. Be on the lookout for how a child might be experiencing different stages of grief, but know that a child won't always move through them one after another after another. With this in mind, understanding common responses to grief and their general progression can help us better understand and make sense of what our child is going through.

Give kids space to process

When helping a child work through grief and loss, give them space to process what they are thinking and feeling. Again, the key is not to fix something or to say just the right thing to make them feel better. Instead, simply listen to your child and give them space to tell you what they are thinking and feeling. Go slow—let them share at a pace that feels comfortable to them, and don't try to influence or shift their experience.

Get more help if needed

It is normal for children to experience grief and loss, and it is normal for these feelings to come and go over time. There may be times when your child is feeling their losses more acutely, and it may not make sense why. If your child is struggling with grief and loss and is having trouble completing normal activities like school or connecting with friends, it might be time to get more help.

I can't say enough about the importance of getting your child counseling with a trauma-informed therapist. I encourage everyone to try counseling. Even if you aren't sure whether your child needs it, it can be helpful to try. If it is hard to connect with your child about their grief and loss and you get the sense that they may need help to talk through what is bothering them, counseling is a great option. What a child can't talk out, they will act out. Getting them the emotional support they need will help them to make sense of their experiences and feelings.

Another option is a support group where your child can be with other children who are adopted or in foster care. Just as adoptive and foster parents need to be in community with other parents who truly get it, kids need community with other kids who understand what they are going through. This is why Replanted organizes small groups for both parents and kids. Children rarely have an opportunity to connect with other kids who are adopted or in foster care, and it is so important for them to be in relationship with others who have had similar experiences. See if there is a support group for kids in your community or faith community. Local counselors may also offer therapy groups for kids that would be an excellent option for them to find support.

DISCUSSION QUESTIONS
- What stuck out to you most as you read this chapter? What did you learn about grief and loss that you didn't know previously?
- What is it like for you to engage your child around their experience of grief and loss? What is your natural reaction?
- What is one step you could take toward offering your presence to your child and providing them with a safe space to process their grief and loss?

10

MENTAL HEALTH PROBLEMS AND MEDICAL ISSUES

All kids get sick and have some level of emotional or behavioral problems during their growing-up years. This is part of what it means to be a kid—growing up can be painful and difficult at times. But sometimes these problems become more serious and parents have to help their child navigate mental health concerns and major medical problems. To be sure, these issues are not unique to adoptive and foster families. Much of the material in this chapter is relevant to all families, regardless of whether children come to the family biologically, through foster care, or through adoption. Still, some unique aspects of the adoption and foster care journey affect how families experience and navigate mental health problems and medical issues.

BLAKE AND SARAH

Blake and Sarah became foster parents a few years after they were married. They had a few foster placements that ended with the child being reunified with their parents, and then they started to foster a sweet four-year-old boy named Adam. They fell in love with him immediately. Although it was a tough adjustment at first, Adam eventually started to feel comfortable in their home and became part of their family.

Blake and Sarah's relationships with Adam's birth parents were rocky. Both of his birth parents struggled with substance use issues, and there was also a history of domestic violence in the home. Blake and Sarah always felt a bit nervous about leaving Adam with them during supervised visits, but they knew this was important for him. Two years after Adam came to live with them, the judge ruled that the birth parents had completed their requirements to have Adam back, and Adam's family was reunified.

Unfortunately, the reunification was short-lived. Blake and Sarah received a call about six months after the reunification and were told that Adam was back in the system, and that the parental rights of the birth parents were likely to be terminated permanently. The birth father had lost his temper and beaten Adam severely, leaving Adam in the hospital with a traumatic brain injury. Because of the traumatic brain injury, Adam had also lost sight in both eyes, and the doctors said it was unlikely that Adam would ever see again.

This was a huge blow to Blake and Sarah. They loved Adam so much, and now their sweet boy had been hurt in a way that should never happen to a child. And because of his traumatic brain injury, Adam had permanent disabilities that would last his entire life. Adam's caseworker asked Blake and Sarah whether they would be open to adopting Adam. After a lot of discussion and prayer, Blake and Sarah agreed. They would adopt Adam and do their best to provide a loving and safe home for him.

Fast-forward two years, and Adam is doing well. He is a fun-loving seven-year-old boy who loves animals and exploring new places. And although Blake and Sarah are so happy to have Adam in their family permanently, parenting has been a struggle, and a big part of the challenges are related to Adam's physical problems and disabilities. Blake and Sarah moved to a different town that had a special school for children who are blind, which meant leaving behind their support system and community. Because of Adam's disability, they are constantly "on"—they feel that they can't ever get a break. And there are lots of follow-up appointments, individual education plans, and doctor's visits. Sometimes Blake and Sarah feel that they need a medical degree just to understand everything. Their marriage took a hit.

Adam's situation is unique, but it paints a picture of some of the difficulties and challenges associated with parenting a child who has major medical problems and mental health issues.

HIGHER LEVELS OF NEED

Because children who are adopted or have been in foster care often have a history of trauma and have lived through very challenging experiences at a young age, they can have higher levels of physical and emotional needs than children who have always lived with their biological families. These may include a medical problem or physical disability, or a mental health problem that requires a course of therapy or medication. I am cautious about generalizations—not all children who are adopted or spent time in foster care will have higher levels of need. But some will—and if your child has a higher level of need, it's good to be prepared and know how to get the help and support you need.

You may know about some of these needs before you decide to adopt a child or take a new foster placement. Before you decide about a new placement, the agency should give you all the information they have. For example, in the case of Blake and Sarah, they knew that Adam had a traumatic brain injury and had lost his eyesight before deciding to adopt him.

This can be uncomfortable to talk about, but adoptive and foster parents need to be honest with themselves about their capacity to parent children who have higher levels of physical or emotional needs. Many factors can come into play when thinking about your capacity, but here are a few questions to consider when thinking about welcoming a child who has higher levels of needs into your family:

- How many other children are you caring for currently? What are their levels of physical and emotional needs? Do you feel as if you have some buffer, or do you already feel maxed out?
- What other commitments do you have on your plate right now? For example, what is your level of work commitment? If there are two parents, are both of you working from home or outside the home? If so, is the work full-time or part-time? How much flexibility do you have with your schedules if your children need you to be around, to take them to appointments, and so on?
- How are you (or each of you) doing physically, emotionally, and spiritually? Do you feel that you are in a good, stable place right now, or are you struggling? How much bandwidth do you (or each of you) have?
- Do you have a good support system around you?

My friend Andrew Schneidler, who is an adoptive dad and lawyer who specializes in helping adoptive families, uses a great illustration of this point that has been helpful for me and many adoptive and foster families. He says that being an adoptive or foster family is like being in a canoe traveling down a river. Suddenly, you see a child, helpless in the river, who looks like they might drown. So you steer your canoe over to the child and help them into the boat. Then you continue down the river, until you see another child in the river. Wanting to help that child as well, you steer your canoe over to the child and help them into the boat too.

You start to travel down the river again, and soon you see yet another child struggling in the river. Wanting to help that child as well, you steer your canoe over to the child and help them into the boat. This time, however, it's harder to get the child into the boat. The canoe is weighed down low into the water, and you work hard to balance the canoe and not let water come in from the side of the canoe. You can do it . . . barely. However, it's not too long before you see yet another child in the water. Wanting to help them as well, you steer your canoe over to the child and try to help them into the boat. This time, however, it doesn't work. Everyone doesn't fit in the canoe, and the collective weight is pushing the boat lower and lower into the water. Water starts to spill in over the side of the canoe, and before you know it, the boat has capsized, spilling you and all the kids out into the water.

The moral of this story is we all have limits in our ability and capacity to care for children. Most parents enter the adoption or foster care journey because they love kids and want to help kids who are in need. This is an awesome motivation, and we need parents who are willing to step into the hard and important work of adoption and foster care. Yet we all have limits to our capacity. There will always be more kids who need help, and saying no to a placement can be hard.

However, if we take on more than our capacity, we won't serve our children or ourselves well. I have seen families who had good intentions but who took on more than they were able and then had to retract their commitments and give the child back. In some cases, their marriage struggled, too, and ended in separation or divorce.

I know we all love kids and want to help as many children as possible. My heart breaks when children are hurt or don't have a loving family to call home. I love it when parents feel moved by God to enter into the hard stories of children, whether through family preservation, reunification, or adoption. But in our mission to love and provide for kids in need, let's also be honest about our capacity and limits, especially when it comes to children who have higher levels of physical and emotional needs. Kids who have higher needs will require more from us—of our time, energy, and resources. Before committing, we need to make sure we have the time, energy, and resources to give.

MEDICAL AND MENTAL HEALTH ISSUES

A few medical and mental health issues are more common among children who are adopted or have spent time in foster care. Children who are adopted (both internationally and domestically) have rates of disability that are about twice as high as the general population.[1] These disabilities include autism; sensory disabilities such as deafness, blindness, and hearing or visual impairments; emotional disturbance such as anxiety disorders and bipolar disorders; intellectual disability; orthopedic impairments; other health impairments; learning disability; speech or language impairment; and traumatic brain injury. A wide range of mental health problems may also be induced or exacerbated by the experiences our children have had, including post-traumatic stress disorder (PTSD), reactive attachment disorder, depression, anxiety, substance use issues, conduct disorder, oppositional defiant disorder (ODD), and fetal alcohol spectrum disorders (FASD).

When considering adopting or fostering a child with physical or emotional limitations, a thorough self-assessment is important. Here are some questions to consider:[2]

- What disabilities are you prepared to handle?
- What physical or emotional challenges are you able to face?
- Do you have the financial resources to care for a child or another child, especially one with disabilities?
- Will your insurance policy cover all the child's physical and emotional issues, preexisting conditions, and required therapies?
- Will your insurance policy adequately cover the necessary healthcare providers?
- Will you be able to find a doctor who is willing and able to provide the level of care the child might require?
- Will your school district be able to support the child's educational needs?
- Have you talked to a parent of a child with a similar condition to help prepare you for the challenges ahead?
- Have you identified resources where you can receive the training necessary to help you support a child with special needs?

HELPING YOUR CHILD

When you have a child who has a medical or emotional problem, how can you advocate for your child to receive the best care and services possible? First, remember that for

many medical and mental health difficulties, help and services are out there. However, you may need to do some work
to ensure that your child receives all the best possible services
available. Here are some important tips for advocating for
your child:[3]

- *Learn all you can about your child's special needs.* It's
  important to learn as much as you can about your child's
  needs. Helpful sources of information include doctors,
  specialists, special education experts, parents of children
  with similar special needs, attorneys, and teachers.
- *Ask lots of questions.* Don't be afraid to be assertive
  and keep asking questions until you get a clear answer.
  Also, document the responses rather than relying on
  your memory.
- *Understand special education law.* The law provides certain rights for individuals with disabilities; you'll want
  to understand the rights that your child has.[4]
- *Try to work with teachers and other providers.* Sometimes it can seem like you are working against teachers
  and other providers to fight for the best care for your
  child. But ultimately, you will need to cooperate with
  teachers and other providers to best serve the needs of
  your child. Try to work collaboratively to come up with
  solutions to meet your child's needs.

Getting your child the very best care may sometimes
require sacrifices from you and the rest of your family. Blake
and Sarah, whose story we heard about at the beginning of
the chapter, decided to move to a different town that had
an amazing school for visually impaired children. Blake and
Sarah had the flexibility and financial resources to do that, but
not every family does.

If providing care for one of your children creates a financial need, some organizations might be able to help. For example, the organization Lifesong for Orphans has matching grants available for pre-adoptive families to cover adoption-related expenses. They also offer post-adoption grants to cover services such as counseling, occupational therapy, and others. Many adoption agencies will know about local resources and support that is available, so be sure to talk with your local agency about these options. If your child is in foster care, most services will be covered by the state. If you are adopting a child from foster care, most children will qualify for adoption assistance or an adoption subsidy. This subsidy can help cover additional needs such as counseling, medication, therapy, and specialists. Be sure to talk with your agency about these options before the adoption is finalized.

There's a balance here that is important to consider. In a perfect world, families would have unlimited resources to be able to provide the very best care for their children with medical or mental health difficulties. However, not all families have this option, because of money or other practical limitations (like a job with a fixed location, or the need to be near family). We are called to do the best we can with the resources we have and the situation we find ourselves in. But there are limits to what we can do, and that can be painful to acknowledge. There is grace here as well—God calls us to do the best we can, and then let that be enough. In one poignant passage of scripture, Paul writes that God told him, "My grace is sufficient for you, for my power is made perfect in weakness" (2 Corinthians 12:9). It's important to do our best and think critically about our ability to care for children with higher levels of needs. But it won't be perfect. Ultimately, we do the best we can and trust God to meet us where we are.

DISCUSSION QUESTIONS
- What stuck out to you most as you read this chapter? What did you learn about medical and mental health issues that you didn't know previously?
- If you are thinking about adopting a child or taking on a new foster placement, what questions would you like to consider as a family regarding your readiness to take on a child who may have special needs?
- What is one step you could take toward advocating for your child so they can get the very best services possible?

Part III

TOOLS AND INTERVENTIONS

11

FELT SAFETY

We all know, even if just on an instinctual level, that physical and emotional safety are foundational to personal growth. It is true for us as adults, and it is true for our children. Think about your own experience. Have you ever felt unsafe in a close relationship? You probably couldn't develop an authentic relationship with that person. If the person was important in your life, the experience might have negatively affected other areas of your life as well. This is a common experience. If we don't feel safe and secure, everything stops. We go into survival mode.

In 1954, psychologist Abraham Maslow came up with an elegant theory that can help us understand why safety and security is so important. Maslow organized our different needs as human beings into a pyramid he called the hierarchy of needs.[1] The hierarchy of needs theory says we have certain needs that are more foundational to our existence—these needs are at the bottom of the pyramid. The needs at the top of the pyramid are important, too, but they build on the needs on the lower part of the pyramid. In other words, we can't pursue the needs at the top of the pyramid until the lower ones are met.

Maslow's hierarchy of needs

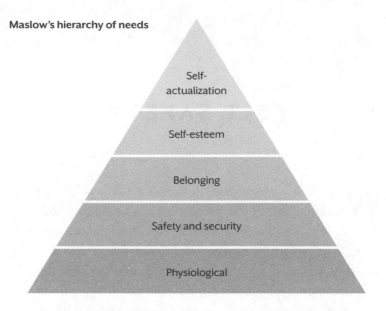

At the very bottom of the pyramid are physiological needs, things like air, water, food, and shelter. This makes sense—if you don't have enough food to eat or a roof over your head, everything else stops until you can get those needs met. They are core and foundational to our survival as human beings. Maslow identified the second level of needs as safety and security, and this is the topic of the current chapter. These needs aren't quite as basic as our physiological needs, but they are close. All human beings have a drive to feel physically and emotionally safe in their environment.

After physiological needs and safety and security, the next levels of needs include belonging (feeling that you fit in and are a part of a group), self-esteem (feeling good about yourself), and self-actualization (reaching your full potential). These are all things we want for ourselves and our children. But if the more foundational need for safety and security isn't met, it's going to be difficult to attain the higher-level needs. That's why working on felt safety is so important for our kids. If we want our children to feel that they belong in our family, they need to feel safe. If we want our children to feel good about themselves, they need to feel safe. If we want our children to reach their full potential, yep, they need to feel safe. In this chapter, we're going to talk about how children feel safe, and how we can help that process.

ASHLEY, BRANDON, AND DEMBE

Ashley and Brandon adopted their son Dembe from Uganda when he was ten years old. In many ways, the transition went well. For the most part, Dembe was a well-behaved boy, and he seemed to fit in well with their family. Ashley and Brandon had two older biological children, Lauren, age fifteen, and Jason, age twelve. Dembe loved playing basketball with Jason in the front driveway, and he enjoyed listening to Lauren play the piano. Dembe also started at their new public school, and his teachers said that Dembe was doing relatively well. It wasn't perfect, but overall, the teachers were happy with how Dembe was doing, especially considering the extent of the adjustment he was having to make with a new school and family.

But a few things concerned Ashley and Brandon. One issue had to do with food. When they cleaned Dembe's room, they would often find old food that Dembe had hidden around the room—for example, they found half-eaten granola bars under his bed and moldy cheese in his closet. Another issue had to do with correction and discipline. When Dembe did something that needed correction and Ashley and Brandon tried to talk to him about it, he would get very upset, start crying, and run to his room and shut the door. Ashley and Brandon tried their best to offer discipline in a kind, caring way, but they could barely start a conversation before Dembe would withdraw and have a meltdown.

When they went to family counseling to explore these issues, they realized that many of Dembe's struggles were related to not feeling safe in his new home or with Ashley and Brandon. Dembe was not consciously aware of this feeling, but it was clear that it was driving some of his behaviors. He had grown up in a very chaotic environment. At the orphanage, it wasn't guaranteed that Dembe would have enough to eat each day. Also, the leaders of the orphanage sometimes got very angry with Dembe over minor issues. Sometimes they even physically abused him by slapping or hitting him when he did something wrong. Given his history, some of Dembe's behaviors started to make more sense. To move forward, Ashley and Brandon would need to work with Dembe to help him get to a point where he felt safe—both physically and emotionally—in his new home.

FEELING SAFE

Adoptive or foster parents sometimes have a tough time understanding why a child doesn't feel safe in their home. Sure, it makes sense why their child wouldn't have felt safe in their previous home. That home might have been chaotic, and there may have been some real dangers there, such as an abusive parent. But now, the adoptive or foster parent might think, the situation is different. The current environment is safe, the child has enough food, the abusive parent is out of the picture, and so on. So why doesn't the child feel safe?

It is a mistake to assume a child will immediately feel safe when taken out of a threatening situation. As the popular book reminds us, our body keeps the score,[2] and it can be hard to turn off the survival response. There is a difference between *knowing* in your head you are safe and *feeling* you are safe. Knowing you are safe is a cognitive process—it involves reasoning and thinking. Feeling you are safe is an emotional process—it involves emotions and the body. It can take a long time in a safe environment before children can feel, deep in their body, that they are safe. For some children who have been hurt or traumatized severely, it may also take work in counseling to get to that point.

Your child may have built up a lifetime of experiences that have shown them the world and the people who are supposed to care for them are not safe. This is their lived experience, and it is supported by data and experiences, some of them traumatic. Your child then reacts to and engages the world based on these experiences. If one day they are suddenly placed in a new, safe environment, they won't automatically change their reactions and behaviors to match their new environment. They were conditioned by the old environment, so that is how they will continue to react. It may take a long time and many new experiences before their conditioning begins to change. Telling children they are safe isn't going to automatically make them feel they are safe. Telling children they are safe and then being a safe person, consistently, day after day, is what will move the needle over time.

Like so many other emotional journeys, the journey to feeling safe isn't always linear. A child may do really well for a while and feel safe in their new environment, and then something can happen that brings the child right back to feeling unsafe. This is a normal part of the process. It doesn't mean your progress is lost or your child is moving in the wrong direction. Sometimes it can seem like your child is taking two steps forward and one step back. This is normal. Healing doesn't always happen in a straight line. If you have experienced a traumatic event—a car accident, physical or sexual assault, or natural disaster—this concept likely rings true for you. Even though the situation has changed and you might know in your head that you are safe, you may not *feel* safe, especially when something reminds you of the past trauma.

HELPING YOUR CHILD FEEL SAFE

What can we do to help our children feel safe? We know that the journey toward feeling safe takes time, but what can we do to help our children along the way?

Consistency and structure

It is helpful to provide a consistent structure in the home. When things are consistent and children can predict what will happen to them in their environment, they feel as if they have more control over their lives and what happens to them, which helps them feel safe. Consistency and structure also decrease the anxiety our children feel about the unknown. Children who are adopted or have spent time in foster care often come from environments that are chaotic and unstructured, so this may be a big change for them. Some children may resist the structure you wish to provide, because it might seem like an imposition. But it's important to stick with it because consistency and structure is one of the most important ways we can help children feel safe.

Consistency and structure can be applied to almost every area of life. For example, if your child struggles to feel safe, don't make any big changes to their environment. Implement and practice daily routines. Try to wake up and go to bed at the same time each day. Go through a morning routine before you send your child off to school. Have a bedtime routine you do every night before your child goes to bed. For example, read a few books, sing a couple songs, and say a prayer to help your child know it is bedtime. Implement fun traditions you do each day or week. Make their day as predictable as possible. For example, maybe you go out to eat at the same restaurant each Sunday after church, or you stop by your favorite donut shop for breakfast on Saturdays. The more you can implement structure and routine in your child's life, the better.

For younger children, create a visual chart that outlines what is happening each day. Print out pictures and apply an adhesive like Velcro to the back so you can create an outline of the activities the child will participate in that day. For example: in the morning, we get ready for school, Mom brings you to school, after lunch the social worker will pick you up for a visit with your birth parents at the foster care agency, the social worker will bring you back to school, Dad will pick you up from school, we will eat dinner together, have playtime, and then you will sleep in your bed tonight. Making the days predictable and outlining what children can anticipate helps create stability and thus decrease anxiety.

Be clear and not vague. Many children don't understand references to time, such as "Mommy will be back this afternoon." Instead, say, "Mommy will pick you up after lunch and you will eat dinner at home with us." That helps a child reference points of the day with clarity. I also recommend printing a "wild card" and letting children know that sometimes things come up in our days and we need to change our schedule slightly. When needed, you can add the wild card and talk about the change. But again, our kids' minds can race with thoughts about their future, so as much as possible, make the schedule predictable to help decrease their anxiety around the unknown.

For parents who are not naturally structured people, this can take some work. It may feel unnatural to have a consistent waketime and bedtime for your child, for example. But if your child is struggling to feel safe in your home, do everything you can to structure their environment as much as possible.

Smooth transitions

One important component of creating a predictable and safe environment for our kids involves helping them with transitions.[3] Has your child ever had a meltdown when you told them it was time for bed or they had to get out of the pool? Transitions are difficult for children, especially those who have experienced trauma and may have difficulties with self-regulation. To help ease transitions, get in the habit of giving children advance notice (for example, "Okay, we are going to play for five more minutes, and then we will read a story and go to bed" or "You can pick two more activities to do on the playground before it's time to leave—which two activities would you like to do?"). Set a countdown timer for children who have difficulty understanding time. When giving your children notice about upcoming transitions, make sure you connect with them and have their attention. It can also be helpful to have them repeat back what is going to happen so you know they heard you ("Okay, honey, what are we going to do in five minutes?"). If your child struggles a lot with transitions, give them multiple advance notices before the transition occurs, such as at ten minutes, five minutes, and one minute.

In addition to softening daily transitions, families often find that larger transitions like the first day of school or moving to a new placement can be stressful for their children.[4] We can work to soften these transitions in similar ways by talking with our children ahead of time about the transition and what will happen. This can lessen the unknowns of a transition, which can create fear. For example, if your child is going to a new school, consider visiting the school together and meeting their teacher beforehand so they know what to expect. Some schools even allow parents to accompany their children on a "practice bus ride" so they can feel more comfortable. If your child has had multiple placements and transitions, helping them create a life book or memory book (with pictures and mementos from their different placements) can help ease the stress and fear from these transitions.

How safe are you?

This can be an uncomfortable topic, but it's important to do a rigorous self-assessment of any behaviors we might be doing as parents that could contribute to our child's not feeling safe. Look, I get it. Parenting is tough. Sometimes our children seem to aggravate us on purpose, and they know exactly what to do to push our buttons. But if we respond in an angry or aggressive manner, it can trigger their old conditioning and put them right back into a place of feeling unsafe. So check in with yourself. How do you respond when you are angry or frustrated with your child? Do you ever lose your temper or raise your voice in an angry manner? When you are angry, are you physically more rough with your child, such as grabbing, pulling, or pushing? Do you ever hit your kids or spank your kids in a hard way? If so, you are likely contributing to your child's feeling unsafe. Seeing a counselor or mental health professional can help you find more effective ways of dealing with your anger.

I saw this while doing trauma counseling with a six-year-old boy who had significant abandonment issues. He had been in counseling with me for almost six months, and at this point he had been separated from his siblings and placed in a new foster home. He was so sweet, but he was struggling to cope with all the loss he had experienced. On one counseling day, he refused to leave. Our session had ended and he did not want to get in the car with his social worker to go home. I knew goodbyes were hard for him. I used all the therapy tricks I knew to support him, and he finally agreed to get in the car if I carried him. So I did. I picked him up and carried him to the car. However, as I was about to place him in his booster seat, he lost it. He started screaming, hitting me, and kicking me in the face. I was frazzled, to say the least.

Here's the thing, though. Responding in a harsh or loud way would have only exacerbated his trauma response. I needed to see that something was triggering him and he needed support. Sure, I could have been firm with him and perhaps he would have stopped. But fear-based parenting will not contribute to felt safety, which is our bigger goal. So I took him back into the office building (because it was the middle of winter), and he ran and hid under my desk. I was shaking. What had just happened? If I'm being honest, I did not want to deal with this. I'm sure many of you can relate. But I needed to press in. He needed me. He needed me to help him self-regulate. He needed to know he was safe. And so we started over. I cleared my schedule and got down on his level to work through all the feelings he was having. We rehearsed him leaving and what feelings that might bring up, and he was able to head home. Phew!

It's also important to consider the extent to which all parts of your child are safe with you. For example, how do you react when your child expresses different emotions, such as sadness, anger, or fear? Are some of these emotions "off-limits" in your home, or do you implicitly discourage them? Also, how safe are you with all the parts of your child's story? Do you feel uncomfortable when your child talks about wanting to find their birth parents, or when your child expresses dreams different from your own? Are you a safe place for your child to discuss issues related to their cultural background and identity? Do you have a subconscious timeline for when you think your child should move beyond their trauma-related behaviors? If you feel uncomfortable seeing or engaging certain issues or emotions in your child, these issues also might be important for you to discuss with a counselor.

Being present and meeting needs over time

Perhaps the most important way to help your child feel safe with you is to consistently be present with them and meet their needs over time. Consistency is key. You are trying to counteract your child's prior conditioning by giving them a new experience with you. They may have been left or abandoned; you are trying to show them you will be present. They may have been physically abused; you are trying to show them you won't hurt them. They may have been emotionally hurt or abused; you are trying to show them you are a safe person with whom they can share their emotions. They may have been neglected; you are trying to show them you will consistently meet their basic needs.

In all these areas, consistently showing up and meeting your child's needs is key. Your child's prior conditioning will not be reworked right away. You are literally rewiring their brain. But little by little, their new experiences with you will be new data and information for them to consider when trying to figure out what to expect from you. Little by little, they will begin to feel more safe and secure in their relationship with you. And that is what we are hoping for as parents.

Expressing love and affection

We can help our children feel safe by consistently expressing love and affection to them. This may seem like a no-brainer,

but parents sometimes struggle with this step, especially if they
are having many negative interactions with their child. Sometimes it can seem like most of the interactions we have with
our children are negative or involve discipline or correction.
It's important to balance those interactions with words and
behaviors that express love and care for our children.

We can express love and affection for our children in many
ways, and my recommendation is to try them all and do them
often. Love and affection can be expressed through words ("I
love you"; "You're my favorite kid in the whole world"), physical touch (hugs, kisses, cuddles), and spending intentional time
together (going to the park or playing together). You might
find other ways to express love and affection to your child.
If affection is hard for you, here are a few suggestions. One
activity I love is called the "weather report." It goes like this:
You and your child take turns giving the weather report using
your hands on each other's back. First you start by saying,
"Let's do an activity called the weather report. There are all
different kinds of weather—it can be sunny, rainy, windy, hur-
ricane season, sleet, and more. What kind of weather would
you like today?" (Have the child respond). "Can I give you
rainy weather on your back?" (Allow the child to respond
because we want to honor their voice). "Is it soft or heavy
rain?" (This question is important for children with sensory
issues who may want softer or harder touch). Then mimic the
weather on their back as they requested. Then have the child
take a turn and give the weather report on your back. It's a
great connection opportunity!

Other ideas include asking permission to apply lotion to
their back, arms, and legs, or brushing their hair. The key here is
to take turns and have your child reciprocate the healthy touch
if they are willing. Touch can play a powerful role in helping

children heal from their trauma experiences.[5] Don't skip this. The important part isn't what exactly you do, but rather that you do it often and in different ways. Kids who have endured very difficult circumstances especially need to know we love them and care for them. We need to remind them, early and often. What is one way that you could show love and affection for your child today? Try it out and see what happens.

Playfulness

Playfulness helps disarm fear,[6] which can improve feelings of safety in our children. Remember that when a child experiences trauma, their brain is affected. When they feel threatened or unsafe, the amygdala, the most primitive part of the brain, can take over, shutting down the prefrontal cortex and the executive functions of their brain. Playfulness can help counteract this process and improve safety. As much as possible, try to be playful when you engage with your child. Even when the interaction seems to be going in a negative direction, playful engagement can sometimes improve safety in the moment and turn the interaction around. For example, Karyn Purvis, who cofounded the Karyn Purvis Institute of Child Development at Texas Christian University, shared a story of a child who demanded a crayon from her. She responded playfully by saying, "Whoa, nelly! Are you asking or telling?"[7] Find your own style, but experiment with playfulness.

ASHLEY, BRANDON, AND DEMBE

Check out this interaction between Ashley and Dembe, whom we met earlier in this chapter, and think about how the interaction might help Dembe feel safer. The setting is the kitchen table, and Ashley wants to talk about finding food in Dembe's room again.

ASHLEY. Hey, buddy, can I talk to you about something?

DEMBE. Uh-huh.

ASHLEY. First off, I want you to know how happy I am to be your mom. I was just thinking about that earlier today, how lucky Daddy and I are to have you as part of our family.

DEMBE. [*smiles*]

ASHLEY. Also, I was doing your laundry today, and I found some half-eaten candy bars in your closet. It's okay—you aren't in trouble. It's just that sometimes leaving food out can attract bugs.

DEMBE. Uh-huh.

ASHLEY. Did you want to keep them for some reason?

DEMBE. Well, in case I get hungry.

ASHLEY. Ah, I get it. So you wanted to have them in case you got hungry?

DEMBE. Yeah.

ASHLEY. I certainly wouldn't want you to go hungry— that's no fun. I want you to know that you can always ask Daddy or me for food when you get hungry. Still, though, it seems like there is something about having some extra food in your room that helps you feel safe, like you've got the food part settled.

DEMBE. Yeah, I just don't want to feel hungry.

ASHLEY. I get that, buddy; I don't like to feel hungry, either. I have an idea. What if we put a little box in your room and you could keep some food in there just in case you got hungry? We could check the box each night before you go to bed, and if it's empty, we could fill it up again. That way, you can always have some food in there, just in case. Does that sound good?

DEMBE. [*nods*]

What do you notice in this dialogue? The issue is about how Dembe is hoarding food. For cleanliness reasons, Ashley and Brandon would prefer Dembe not keep old food in his room. But the issue is deeper than that. As I noted earlier in the chapter, in the orphanage where he grew up, Dembe didn't always get his basic needs met, including having enough food. So it makes sense that Dembe would hoard food, even though his new reality is a full pantry. He may know this intellectually, but he doesn't feel it yet emotionally. And his emotions, such as fear, are driving his behavior.

Instead of punishing Dembe for hoarding food again, Ashley tries to address the underlying issue—Dembe doesn't feel safe or secure that he will always have enough food to eat. On this point Ashley aligns with Dembe—she doesn't want Dembe to feel hungry, either. She suggests a solution that might help Dembe feel safer—to keep some extra food in a box in his room. Note that this might require an adjustment on Ashley and Brandon's part—they might prefer Dembe keep no food in his room whatsoever, or only eat his food in the kitchen. But in this case, Ashley is willing to be flexible to help Dembe feel safe. Over time, keeping food in a box in his room may no longer be necessary, but right now it is a loving action that can help Dembe on his journey to feeling safe in his new home

DISCUSSION QUESTIONS

- What stood out to you most as you read this chapter? What did you learn about safety that you didn't know previously?
- Did anything come up for you personally as you reflected on your sense of safety as a parent? Is there any personal work you need to do to be a safe parent for your child?
- What is one practical step you could take toward helping your child feel safer in your home?

12

CONNECTION

We all want to connect with our kids. We want to develop strong bonds with our children that stand the test of time. You might see families playing together at the park or kids excited about movie night with the family and wonder, How do families get to that place? Our lived experience is often much different from what we see in the movies or the ideal we have in our head. Sometimes it seems that our kids don't want anything to do with us. And if we're honest, sometimes we don't want to connect with our kids. Maybe we feel that we don't have anything in common, or they are into "weird" stuff that holds no interest for us. Maybe we have lived so long in the world of adults that we have forgotten how to play. Whatever it is, connecting with our kids is something we might think should be easy, but it often isn't. This chapter explores some helpful strategies for connecting with our kids.

HANNAH, RYAN, AND ANGELICA
Hannah and Ryan adopted Angelica when she was eight months old. Angelica was their only child. For Hannah, connecting with a baby was easy. She had done a lot of babysitting growing up and had also spent a lot of time with her nieces

and nephews and volunteering at the church nursery. Connecting with a baby was like second nature to her. But Ryan felt differently. He didn't have as much experience with babies, so it was tough for him to connect. It was almost like he didn't know what to do.

As Angelica grew older, their experiences with connection continued to shift. When Angelica was a toddler, Ryan still found it challenging to connect with her. Ryan was a more serious person, and it was tough for him to let his hair down and be silly and play. The ways that Angelica wanted to play didn't make sense to him, and he struggled to connect at her level. For example, one time he got frustrated because they were trying to play a game and Angelica kept making up her own rules.

When Angelica started school, Ryan found it easier to connect with her because her activities were more structured. Ryan helped with homework, and he enjoyed kicking the soccer ball around together in the backyard. However, as Angelica got older, Hannah realized she was having more difficulty connecting with her daughter. As a stay-at-home mom, Hannah found that most of her interactions with Angelica were correcting her or trying to get her to do certain things, like brush her teeth and clean up her room. Hannah would get so frustrated with Angelica that she didn't have any energy to play and connect as they did when Angelica was younger.

THE IMPORTANCE OF CONNECTION

Connection is one of the most important aspects of parenting, but it can also be challenging. Part of the problem is that we sometimes think it should come naturally—that connection should "just happen." Connection does "just happen" for some parents, but this is not everyone's experience, and probably not most people's experience. Most of us have to work on this aspect of our relationship with our child. We have to put in some effort, or do things that may not be comfortable, to connect with our child and meet them where they are.

It's worth putting in the work, however, because developing a strong bond with our child through connection is one of the best ways to help them heal and grow, especially if they have experienced trauma in their past. Playfulness helps disarm the fear response, promote attachment, and build social competence.[1] Playfulness also produces warmth and trust between a child and their caregivers.[2] We might think that to heal from trauma, we have to spend all our time doing deep work processing what happened to us. This can be important. But playfulness and having positive interactions with our child consistently over time is just as important.

Keep in mind that building a connection with your child takes time. If you have just received a new placement, it's normal for connection to be difficult at first. You are getting used to each other, and the adjustment can be tough for everyone. Give yourself grace if you don't feel love and affection for your child immediately. And give your children grace if they don't feel love and affection for you right away. This is a new relationship, and the process of building connections is slow. Keep at it, and be consistent.

For some parents, the relationship between you and your child may be so sour that it feels like neither of you want to connect with each other. If you are in this place, give yourself and your child grace. Try some of the suggestions in this chapter, and see if something shifts.

HOW TO CONNECT WITH YOUR CHILD

We know that connecting with our children is important, especially for kids who may have experienced trauma and other difficult things in their upbringing so far. But how do we do it? If we are struggling to connect with our child, what can help us move forward?

Remember how to play

In the previous chapter, we discussed how playfulness can help build a sense of felt safety. Playfulness is critical for building connection as well. But many adults have forgotten how to play. At most workplaces or other places where we interact mainly with adults, things are serious. People talk in even tones—not too loud and not too soft. Silliness or rambunctiousness is discouraged. Jokes might be okay if they are particularly clever, but overall, they tend to be frowned upon. There is serious work to be done—there isn't much time for play or foolishness.

Parents try to use this serious interpersonal stance to relate to their kids, and it doesn't work. You miss each other because you are operating on different wavelengths. You might even get frustrated with your child when they are silly, or loud, or make a mess with their toys. Or you might get bored playing with your child. But silliness and playfulness are a big part of how kids connect. And as the adults, it's up to us to move toward our children and connect on their level. A big part of this "moving toward" is remembering how to play.

What would it look like if you took yourself less seriously? Could you let your hair down and be silly? Could you yell and shout? Could you make a mess and not get frustrated about it? Could you see something getting broken and be okay with it since you had a great time? If the answer to these questions is no, you might have some work to do in remembering how to play. Sometimes it helps adults to think back and reflect on what they were like as kids. When you were a child, what activities and toys were you into? What brought you joy? Could you reconnect with some of those experiences as an adult?

Fill the trust bank

If you want to connect with your child, you need to increase the number of positive interactions you have. Sometimes parents get into trouble because most of the interactions they have with their child involve something negative—like discipline, correction, or saying no. These interactions aren't bad per se—every parent has to discipline and correct their child and say no. But this becomes a problem when the negative interactions outnumber and overwhelm the positive interactions. Often this happens without us even realizing it.

My friend Daren Jones, associate director of the Karyn Purvis Institute of Child Development, helpfully describes this by saying that all kids have a trust bank.[3] Every time you have a positive interaction with your child, it's like making a deposit in their trust bank. Every time you have a negative interaction with your child, it's like making a withdrawal. You have to build up positive interactions with your child so you have enough "money in the bank" when the negative interactions inevitably happen. Also, you might think that the trust bank starts at zero when you adopt a child or they enter a placement with you because you haven't had any prior interactions with them. For most of our kids, however, their trust bank starts in the negative because of prior negative experiences with caregivers. This makes it even more important to build up positive interactions with your child, and to do so consistently. Even if you are frustrated or angry with your child, make sure to keep making deposits in their trust bank.

Now you might be wondering, How do I put positive inter-actions in my child's trust bank when our relationship is in a bad place? Here are a couple of suggestions:

1. *Praise and affirmation.* We often praise our children's *behavior.* For example, "Thanks for cleaning up your room. I love it when you do that." Or, "Thanks for listening the first time." And often we do this because we want more of this good behavior. But when it comes to praise and affirmation that builds relational trust, focus on character traits, not behaviors. For example, "You are a very thoughtful friend. You care deeply about your family. I love your goofy side. I love how much energy you have." Give your child praise and affirmation about *who* they are and not *how* they are behaving.

2. *Yeses.* Have you seen the movie *Yes Day?* In the movie, the parents decide to give their children a "yes day," where the parents say yes to all the kids' requests (with certain parame-ters around things like spending money). Do you know what happens? The family has a blast together. Now, you obviously can't do "yes days" every day, but are there times in the day where you can give simple yeses? Maybe your child asks for some bubble gum. Say yes—maybe even give them two pieces! Maybe your child wants to help with dinner. Is there a simple way they can help out so you can say yes and connect? Many of our kids did not receive yeses from caregivers. For example, a baby may have cried for a parent and no one came. They didn't receive yeses for their needs, and therefore nos can be triggering. A great way to build connection and trust is by responding with yes.

Engage at the child's level
Engaging with your child on their level—literally, in a physical posture—is a simple suggestion, but parents don't often think

about it. If you have a toddler, for example, it's hard to connect when they are sitting on the ground and you are standing six feet in the air. There's just too much distance between you. Plus, it can be scary if you are a little person and a big person is towering over you. Instead, as much as possible, get down on your child's level. If your child is sitting or lying down, get down on the ground as well. If your child is crawling around, get down on your hands and knees and follow suit. Lower the distance between you and your child, and you will make it easier to connect. When your child is playing, try getting down on the ground and staying at the child's level. How does this small change affect your connection with your child?

Soft ... voice, face, body language

Children, especially young children, are easily scared and startled. They are little, and the world around them is big. It makes sense that they get scared. And some of our children may have had bad experiences with threatening adults, which can make startling or loud voices a trigger for them. Some parents are naturally loud, have a stern look to their face, or make big motions with their body language. When you are engaging with children, especially babies and small children, it's helpful to be soft. Use a soft voice—lower your volume and use a playful or singsong tone. Have a soft face—smile and laugh a lot, and be careful of angry or stern expressions toward your child. Finally, have soft body language—think about using welcoming body language such as open arms, hugging, patting, and rubbing. Remember ... soft voice, soft face, soft body language.

Reflective play

Some parents tell me they don't know how to play with a small child. Luckily, playing with a small child isn't rocket science.

One simple strategy is reflective play, where you follow along with what the child is doing. If the child is playing with blocks and building a tower, join in and help with the tower. If the child is playing with a doll, join in and play with a doll. If the child is pushing around a car or truck, follow their lead and do the same thing. In this way, you let the child lead and follow along with what they are doing and are interested in. Then, reflect how they are playing instead of asking questions. For example, "The car is going really fast," or "You are doing such a great job taking care of your baby doll." This shows your child you are focused on them and that their voice matters.

The same strategy can be used when babies start to talk and make noises. When a baby makes a cooing sound, make the same cooing sound back. If they say ba-ba-ba, say ba-ba-ba back. Kids love this back-and-forth, and it can be a great way to connect with a very young child. It also helps the child understand they are relational and have an impact on you because you are repeating what they are saying.

Follow their interests

Parents sometimes struggle to connect with their children, especially as they grow up, because they might not be interested in the same things. You might be into music, for example, but your child is into sports. Or you might be into studying and reading books, but your child is into building and fixing things. There can be a disconnect if your interests don't line up.

It's important to follow your child's interests, whatever they are. This doesn't mean you have to throw out your old interests or throw yourself completely into their interests, but it does mean actively supporting them in their pursuits. Children go through numerous phases as they grow up and explore different things. This is part of growing up—children try out different activities while learning who they are and what things they are good at and enjoy doing. Our job as parents is to follow their lead and support their exploration, even if we aren't personally interested in the activity. The goal of parenting isn't to create a person in our image, or to have more fun ourselves. The point of parenting is to help our kids discover who they are and become the best version of themselves. When done well, parenting is a selfless act.

HANNAH, RYAN, AND ANGELICA

Check out this excerpt from a family therapy session with Hannah, Ryan, and Angelica (whom we met in the beginning of this chapter) as the therapist tries to coach Ryan in connecting with Angelica, who is sixteen months old. (Hannah was present but did not speak during this part of the session.)

THERAPIST. Okay, Ryan, what do you notice about Angelica right now?

RYAN. Well, she is sitting down on the floor, playing with her blocks. And she looks relatively happy.

THERAPIST. Yeah, that's great, Ryan, I see those things too. Now, let's say you were wanting to connect with your daughter, what do you think you would normally do?

RYAN. Well, I'd probably see if she wanted to read a book or go for a walk, or something like that.

THERAPIST. Gotcha. Now how do you think you would go about doing that? I mean, how would you know if she wanted to read a book or go for a walk?

RYAN. Well, she can't really talk yet. I guess I would ask her anyways, and then if it seemed like she wasn't upset or crying, I would grab a book and read it to her, or get her ready to go for a walk.

THERAPIST. Got it, that makes sense. It sounds like you would take the lead there and kind of assume that if she wasn't upset, she would want to do those things.

RYAN. Yeah, I suppose that's right.

THERAPIST. Now, I don't think there's necessarily anything wrong with taking the initiative to connect with your daughter in that way. Most kids like to read books and go for walks. But another way to connect might be to observe what your daughter is doing right now and try to join her in that. Let's go back to your initial observation about Angelica—that she was sitting on the floor and playing with blocks. Would you be willing to reflect exactly what Angelica is doing—in other words, get down on the floor with her and play blocks with her?

RYAN. Sure, I can do that. [*sits on the floor with Angelica and starts to play blocks*]

THERAPIST. Great, now keep on reflecting what Angelica is doing, and see how that feels.

RYAN. You're stacking the yellow block on the blue block. You're doing a great job being focused, Angelica.

Can you see how Ryan's initial reaction when trying to connect with his daughter is to come up with an activity and have her do it with him—even though she is already happily doing something else? This can be especially true for parents of teens. Perhaps your teen is playing video games and you try to connect with them by asking them to turn off the game and come talk. Again, it's not wrong to initiate activities with your children—this is fine to do. But when trying to connect with your child, try getting down on their level and reflecting what they are doing—which is what the therapist was trying to coach Ryan to do. Maybe it's time for you to pick up the video game controller and join your child.

DISCUSSION QUESTIONS

- What stuck out to you most as you read this chapter? What did you learn about connecting with your child that you didn't know previously?
- Is it tough for you to remember how to play? Does playfulness come naturally for you or is it uncomfortable? What is something you could do to connect with your inner child?
- What is one practical suggestion about connecting with your child that you would like to try today?

13

CORRECTION

When I talk with foster and adoptive parents about their parenting questions, the most common issues and problems involve correction. The concerns vary, but at some level, they boil down to this: the child is doing a behavior that is concerning or harmful (hitting, self-harm, yelling) or is *not* doing a behavior that the parent would like them to do (homework, brushing their teeth, cleaning their room), and the parent is struggling to get the child to either stop doing the harmful behavior or start doing the positive behavior consistently. Of all the concerns I hear, this is the most consistent, and often the one causing the most confusion and frustration. Now, these are common issues for all parents, but correction has particular challenges when a child has a history of trauma. Parents with biological children sometimes find that the correction strategies they used with those children don't work with children who have been adopted or spent time in foster care. How can we take a trauma-informed approach to correction?

All children need correction, discipline, and teaching. That's an important task of parenting. But I commonly hear that the correction doesn't seem to work. The parent might employ a strategy like a time-out, spanking, or token system, but it doesn't change the child's behavior. So they try several strategies, and when none of them seem to work, the parent gets more and more frustrated. Another problem is that the process of correction seems miserable for both parent and child. The child might get very upset, perhaps even throw a fit, which causes yet another problem for the parent to manage. The parent, too, can get angry and lose their cool, sometimes behaving as badly as the child. Your teen may blatantly disrespect you or ignore your requests. Yelling matches may ensue. Both parent and child might leave the interaction angry and frustrated, thinking there must be a better way.

Before we get too far into the details of effective correction, it's important to understand how trauma influences the brain and behavior. When you can view your child's behavior through a trauma lens, you may begin to see the behavior as a deficit and not as defiance. So how does trauma affect the brain? Recall from chapter 5 that the part of our brain called the amygdala is responsible for survival. If we were out for a hike and encountered a bear, the amygdala would kick in and tell us whether we should run, fight the bear, or freeze and play dead—the fight, flight, or freeze response. When the amygdala gets involved, it turns off many other areas of our brain, especially those in the frontal lobe responsible for higher cognitive functions like language, emotional regulation, impulse control, motor function, and executive functioning (e.g., working memory, self-control, flexible thinking). Our moral compass is housed there as well. Maybe you see the connection already. For children with a history of trauma, the part of the brain responsible for helping them talk, cope with their feelings, and remain flexible in their thinking has been compromised. This is why our kids may have longer-than-average temper tantrums, trouble staying on task, and difficulty verbalizing their feelings. Some of you may be thinking, "But my child isn't in a traumatic situation right now." And this is true, but the body keeps the score.[1]

The good news is, there is a better way forward. I don't want to get your hopes up—there isn't a panacea or simple strategy that will make correction and discipline easy. There isn't a one-size-fits-all approach that will work with every single child. But you can try some principles and strategies to make the process of correction more successful for children affected by trauma, and perhaps even deepen the relationship between you and your child rather than tear it apart.

IMANI AND SARAH

Imani was a single mom who adopted Sarah when she was three years old. To say that it was a challenging adjustment would be an understatement. Using Imani's words, Sarah was "wild." She would career through the house, knocking over and breaking things. She wouldn't listen to Imani, even about dangerous things like running in the street or talking with strangers. Imani tried to engage in discipline softly, but soon she would escalate when Sarah didn't respond to her corrections. Sometimes Imani even found herself yelling and screaming, losing her temper with Sarah. Afterward, she would feel embarrassed about losing her cool, but she couldn't help it. It was a combination of anger, fear, and frustration, and it just boiled over sometimes.

Imani tried everything she could think of and read about when it came to correction and discipline. She tried time-outs, spanking, and even a complicated token reward system that got great reviews online. Nothing seemed to work. When Imani tried to implement consequences for Sarah, they just seemed to escalate and increase her negative behaviors. Finally, Imani took Sarah to family counseling. She was at the end of her rope.

Have you ever felt like Imani when trying to correct and discipline your kids? You try everything, but nothing seems to work. You ask around to see what other parents are doing, and you try their ideas as well, but what works for their kid and situation doesn't seem to work for you. If you're feeling frustrated about correction and discipline, you are not alone. This is one of the most difficult parts of parenting for everyone, and as noted earlier, unfortunately there isn't an easy, one-size-fits-all answer. In what follows, I walk through some principles and strategies that many parents have found helpful. My hope is some of these ideas can help transform your interactions around correction to something, well, less terrible.

KEYS TO CORRECTION

Let's dive into a few key principles and guidelines that can shape how we correct and offer discipline in a helpful way. These ten principles are applicable to all children, but may be especially useful for children who have experienced trauma in their history.

Key 1: Check in with yourself before engaging in correction or discipline

Sometimes I see parents try to discipline their kid for having a temper tantrum, and the adult is so mad it looks like they are having a temper tantrum themselves. This strategy won't work. You need to be able to regulate and calm yourself before correcting or disciplining your child. The process of correction is relational—if you are not regulated, your child is likely to respond in turn and the situation will escalate. If you are feeling too upset, it's okay to take a break (if you are married, perhaps your spouse can tag in). When you engage with your child, try as much as possible to have a calm voice and a calm face. From your regulated and calm state, you can then help your child regulate themselves. And remember, your child needs help with this. Trauma impairs the area of the brain that helps our children regulate. They need us to model regulation, and they need grace. This is tough to do! Most of us don't mean to lose our tempers with our kids, and we have every intention to remain calm in these situations. It's hard work. Working on self-awareness and being able to pause and check in with ourselves when we notice our own feelings escalating is key.

Key 2: Stay connected while engaging in correction and discipline

Many parents, when they engage in correction and discipline, create distance between themselves and the child. The time-out is a perfect example of this. When a parent gives a time-out, they often send the child to their room. This kind of separation can feel triggering for kids who have experienced trauma or neglect. Instead, as much as possible, try to stay connected while correcting or disciplining. One example of this is a "time-in" as opposed to a time-out. In this strategy, you stay near the child for the time-in while they attempt to regulate and reflect on what went wrong. Instead of sending the child to their room, stay with the child and talk about what happened and what they could do differently. Stay engaged with your child as they do the alternative behavior—for example, instead of sending the child to clean their room, go with the child and clean the room together.

Key 3: Avoid punitive and consequence-oriented correction

Punitive and consequence-oriented correction can activate the trauma response in the brain, so these strategies are less effective for children who have experienced trauma. Fear-based parenting strategies simply do not work with children who have trauma histories. Punitive and consequence-oriented approaches keep the amygdala, or "fight, flight, or freeze" part of the brain, turned on.

Instead of giving a consequence ("If you don't set the table, no video games for a week"), try to work with the child to do the adaptive behavior ("Let's set the table together"). By modeling the adaptive behavior and role-playing it, you are creating muscle memory in the child's brain so they will be more likely to respond this way in the future. Modeling adaptive behavior can be done only when the child has returned to a regulated state. We can't do teaching or reasoning when a child is upset. They won't be able to hear us—physically or emotionally.

Key 4: Focus on teaching, not compliance

Many parents get into a state of mind where they are focused on compliance. With compliance, the goal is to get my kid to do what I tell them to do . . . right away. When we get locked into this mindset, we forget the overarching goal of parenting, which is to help children learn how to operate in the world. The goal of correction and discipline is to help our kids function better and be self-sufficient, happy, contributing members of society. Keep this goal in front of you always.

You could begin by thinking about yourself and how you learn best. Is it with someone screaming at you and sending you to your room? Probably not. Someone sticking with you, remaining calm, staying connected, and showing you how to do something is more effective. When correcting, one great teaching strategy is to have the child do a redo. This means you give the child an opportunity to "redo" the behavior that got them in trouble in the first place. This creates a muscle memory in the child—when they are in the same situation in the future, the alternative behavior will likely come to their mind. Karyn Purvis, the co-creator of the Trust-Based Relational Intervention, once said that we can be in such a hurry to give consequences that we forget we are teaching a child how to do life.[2] Our children don't have as much life experience as we do, nor do they have fully developed brains. Remember this the next time things derail with your child, and give yourself and your child grace.

Key 5: Help the child regulate and calm down first

When children are in a dysregulated state (e.g., upset, crying, flushed face), they are unlikely to be thinking clearly enough to respond positively to correction and discipline. It's not effective to engage with them on this level when they are dysregulated, because the thinking part of their brain is being overwhelmed by their feelings and physical reactions. Instead, focus on helping them calm down and regulate their emotions before engaging in correction and discipline. Then, when they are feeling calm, you can engage in the correction or discipline you have planned.

Key 6: Say yes to feelings, even if you are saying no to a behavior

This principle is based on a teaching from neuropsychiatrist Dan Siegel and parenting expert Tina Payne Bryson.[3] When a child does something we don't want them to do, we often shut them down—both the behavior and the feeling. For example, if a child gets mad and punches their brother, we immediately jump in and send the child to their room. But if we're not careful, the child might learn that some feelings aren't okay. In this example, they might learn that feeling angry isn't okay. Instead, validate their feelings even as you are saying no to the behavior. For example, you might affirm the child's anger ("It looks like you are angry, and that's okay") even as you teach the behavior is not okay ("When we're angry, we might feel like hitting something, but it isn't okay to hit your brother"). We might even offer an alternative ("What else could we do when we get angry?").

Key 7: Don't make a mountain out of a molehill

This might seem like an easy one, but when we get into it with our kids, we can get carried away and lose sight of the bigger picture. Before we know it, we are grounding them for a year for not eating all their vegetables. When you are engaging in discipline and correction, make sure the correction fits the behavior. You can even ask yourself a question like, In the grand scheme of things, how big of a deal was the behavior, from one to ten? For married couples, this is a great time to check in with your spouse as well. If your spouse wasn't in the middle of the situation, they might have more perspective and can help you come up with a correction that better fits the scope of the behavior.

Key 8: Share power with your children when engaging in correction and discipline

This one might seem a little strange, so let me walk you through it. When a parent engages in correction or discipline, they are usually in charge. Like a judge, they administer the punishment from on high. But if we are really in the business of teaching our children, it can be more effective to cultivate a collaborative relationship when correcting or disciplining. For example, one technique I love to use with kids is called "two choices." Let's say you want your child to pick up their room, but they don't want to. You give them two choices: "You can pick up your toys now and have a snack, or would you like me to play with you for five more minutes, and then we can pick up the toys together?" Both options are ultimately acceptable, but by giving the child two choices, you make correction more collaborative and share power with them. This is especially helpful because you are maintaining your authority as the parent (by providing two choices you are okay with), but you are also giving your child a voice by allowing them to choose the option they'd prefer. Giving your child a voice and filling their trust bank with yes opportunities helps a child heal from their trauma experiences. Remember, when giving two choices, both options should be positive. So saying something like "You can either pick up the toys now or lose screen time tonight" is not what we are going for. Keep the options positive.

Another example is the compromise. Some parents resist compromising with their children, but it's an effective strategy for shaping behavior. And like the two choices technique, it shares power with the child and reduces resistance. For example, if you want your child to go to bed and they don't want to, offer a compromise ("Okay, how about we do a compromise? What if I read you one more story that you can choose, and then we will go to bed?"). Some parents don't like compromising, because it feels like losing or giving up, but this is not a problem if our goal is teaching, not compliance. Involving our children in their decisions through techniques like compromise is a helpful way to teach. Plus, negotiating a compromise is similar to real life. We ask for compromises all the time as adults, so it's great to teach kids to ask for what they need or want and see what sort of response they get.

Another example is coaching problem-solving. For example, two kids are fighting over a toy. As parents, we often jump into action, take the toy away, and try to teach with a *verbal* lesson. For example, "If you can't share, then neither of you can have the toy." Instead, coach kids through the problem they are trying to solve—it's a great teaching opportunity. You may say something like "It sounds like you both want the toy. I wonder whether you can figure out how to solve this problem. What could each of you do?" Then, talk through all the possible scenarios to solve the problem. This helps them identify things like taking turns, sharing, or maybe setting a timer so each child gets the same amount of time with the toy. This sort of collective problem-solving can be a great lesson that sets them up to solve future problems more independently.

One helpful model for sharing power with your children (especially teenagers) when engaging in correction is the collaborative and proactive solutions model by psychologist Russ Greene.[4] This collaborative problem-solving model has three steps: The first is empathy—the parent gathers information in order to understand the child's concerns ("I noticed that you sometimes have difficulty putting your phone away during virtual learning—what's up?"). It's important to keep asking questions and drill down to the real issues ("My friends are texting me and I want to stay connected"). Keep asking questions until your child has no further issues to share ("So you want to stay connected to your friends, anything else?"). The second step is to define the problem or concern from your perspective ("I'm concerned that you are missing important information from the class and will fall behind if you aren't focused"). The third step is to invite the child to collaboratively solve the problem with you ("I wonder whether there is a way to stay connected with your friends and focus on your schoolwork"). Let the child lead with possible options and serve as a guide. The goal is to find a solution that is realistic *and* mutually satisfactory.

Key 9: Use positive reinforcement

A system where children gain something they want for doing a desired behavior is more effective than giving children a consequence for *not* doing the desired behavior. Some parents even come up with creative systems that reward various behaviors they want the child to learn to do. When my husband Josh was little, for example, his parents set up a token system to encourage him to do things like brush his teeth and make his bed. Because he had not yet developed these habits, he needed the rewards to encourage him to do the behavior. After a while, however, he was able to do the behavior without the rewards. I am happy to report that he still brushes his teeth twice a day! (We're still working on making the bed.)

When implementing a token or other reward system, make sure the things you are trying to have your child do are achievable given their level of development. You don't want to set up your child for failure. If you are just starting out, you may need to lower the bar for what you expect from them so they are able to have some wins.

Key 10: Have a short memory

It can be very challenging to not hold a child's past behaviors over their head, but when we engage in correction about a behavior and resolve the issue, we need to leave it in the past. It's not helpful to remember and remind the child of their poor behavior when we have already addressed it and moved on. Think about how you feel when you mess up in your marriage or another relationship or at work and someone is constantly reminding you about your failure. It can sour the relationship and make you feel guilty, embarrassed, ashamed, or angry. The same is true for our kids. Leave it in the past and move forward. We don't want to keep driving the parenting car looking in the rearview mirror at all our children's mistakes. We all make mistakes—giving grace and repairing relationships is what is most important. Parenting involves lots of back-and-forth between correction, teaching, and forgiveness. That last step is key.

Physical discipline is not effective

You may have noticed something missing from the discussion about principles for correction—I haven't talked about physical discipline. There is a reason for that—I do not recommend physical discipline of any kind, including spanking, hitting, striking, or whipping. These kinds of physical discipline are not effective at teaching children how to behave, and they can re-traumatize children who have experienced physical and emotional abuse in their past. Physical discipline is fear-based, and research has shown that it is not effective and has long-term consequences for children. For example, children who were spanked had more behavioral problems over time, including increased aggression, antisocial behavior, and disruptive behavior in school.[5] Alan Kazdin, a Yale University psychology professor and director of the Yale Parenting Center and Child Conduct Clinic, puts it this way: "You cannot punish out these behaviors that you do not want. . . . There is no need for corporal punishment based on the research. [By making a case against spanking,] we are not giving up an effective technique. We are saying this is a horrible thing that does not work."[6]

Furthermore, for most foster parents, physical discipline or punishment is absolutely not allowed—you can have your foster license removed for such behaviors. So even if your parents used physical discipline with you, even if you thought it was effective, cut physical discipline out of your parenting.

There just isn't any place for it, especially with children who are adopted or in foster care. If you or another parent relies on physical discipline, there are many good resources available to help caregivers learn new, healthy, and effective habits for correcting children. I urge you to reread and reflect on the ten keys to correction described in this chapter, and to return to them often.

IMANI AND SARAH

Check out this dialogue between Imani and Sarah (whom we met earlier in this chapter) after Sarah's refusal to pick up her toys and get ready for bed. See if you can pick out the principles for good correction that Imani uses.

> IMANI. Okay, Sarah, it's time for bed. Let's pick up our toys and start heading upstairs.

> SARAH. [*starts crying*] But I don't wanna go to bed. I'm not going.

> IMANI. [*sits down with Sarah on her level*] Ah, Sarah, it sounds like you're mad about having to go to bed, and that's okay. It's tough to stop playing when you're having fun.

> SARAH. I wanna play more!

> IMANI. I get that you want to keep playing, but it's time for bed. I'll give you two choices: we can either clean up our toys now and go read a story, or keep playing for five minutes and then pick up our toys. What would you like to do?

> SARAH. Keep playing!

> IMANI. Okay, so your choice is to keep playing for five minutes, and then pick up our toys?

> SARAH. Yes.

IMANI. Okay, I'm going to set a timer here so both of us know how much time is left. What are we going to do when the timer goes off?

SARAH. Clean up the toys.

IMANI. What would you like to play with?

What correction principles do you notice in this dialogue?

DISCUSSION QUESTIONS

- What stood out to you most as you read this chapter? What did you learn about correction and discipline that you didn't know previously?
- What have you noticed about yourself when you engage in correction and discipline with your child? What comes up for you? What behaviors trigger you the most? When is it most difficult for you to remain calm and composed?
- Which of the principles for effective correction did you find most helpful? Which of the principles do you think will be most challenging to implement in your family?

14

EMOTIONAL REGULATION

In the previous chapter, we discussed the importance of helping your child regulate their emotions first, before engaging in correction and discipline. A dysregulated child won't be able to learn or take in anything you are trying to say. And this is especially true for children affected by trauma. When they feel threatened or upset, the amygdala part of the brain that is responsible for survival can take over, and it can shut down the frontal lobe, which is responsible for emotional regulation and executive functioning.

Your child needs to get back to baseline before your lessons have a chance to sink in. But you might be thinking, "Well, that's great, but that's my child's whole problem! When they get upset, it's impossible to calm them down, and we never get anywhere." This is a common problem, one we'll dig into deeper in this chapter. Kids tend to have big emotions. How can we help our children regulate their emotions and express them in an acceptable way?

DONALD AND AVERY

See if you can relate to this story about Donald and his son Avery. Donald and his wife Carolyn have been foster parents for several years, and they recently got a new placement, Avery.

Like many kids his age, five-year-old Avery has big feelings. When he is happy, you can feel the joy radiating from his face. When he is angry, you can almost see the flames coming out of his ears. He yells, screams, and gets destructive. (Think the Anger character from the movie *Inside Out*.) When Avery is sad, he cries and wears his emotions on his sleeves. His feelings are big and they last for a long time.

There's nothing wrong with having big feelings and expressing them. (In fact, our tendency to not express our emotions as freely as we grow older can lead to problems.) Carolyn and Donald don't mind that Avery has big feelings, but sometimes the way he expresses them can cause difficulties. Avery also has trouble calming down and self-soothing.

One Saturday morning, Donald took Avery to the grocery store while Carolyn caught up on some much-needed sleep. It started out as a fun outing, but when they got to the grocery store, Avery saw many items that he wanted—Corn Pops cereal, Twizzlers, and chocolate milk, just to name a few. Armed with his knowledge about compromises, Donald told Avery that he could pick out one item from the store, as long as it was under ten dollars. This seemed to work at first—Avery chose orange Gatorade and they put it in the cart together. But then they passed the cereal aisle and Avery also wanted the Corn Pops. Donald reminded Avery about their agreement— he could choose one item from the store—and that's when the meltdown started. Avery started to cry and soon escalated to yelling, screaming, hitting Donald, lying on the ground in the cereal aisle, and knocking a bunch of cereal boxes to the floor. Donald was unable to calm Avery down, and they ended up having to leave the store and go home, leaving their half-filled shopping cart in the cereal aisle.

EMOTIONAL REGULATION

I'm sure many of us have had similar experiences—our children are experiencing big emotions, and it's difficult to help them calm down. If a two-year-old has a temper tantrum and can't calm down, we generally chalk it up to normal toddler behavior, and maybe try to put them down for a nap. But if a five-, ten-, or fifteen-year-old has a temper tantrum and can't calm down, they still might need a nap, but ideally, we'd like to provide them with tools to help them regulate their emotions. That's what this chapter is about.

Emotional regulation isn't something a person is born with. It's not something you either have or don't have. Emotional regulation is a skill that takes practice, just like riding your bicycle or completing math problems. Many children who are adopted or in foster care may not have had emotional regulation modeled to them by their primary caregivers, and healthy emotional regulation may not have been a focus in their home growing up. Plus, as we've discussed, trauma impairs the part of our child's brain responsible for emotional regulation, making it even harder. But the good news is it's never too late to start learning to regulate your emotions. Even older children and adults can learn these new skills.

Modeling emotional regulation for our kids is key. If we lose our temper or have difficulty managing our emotions, our children will learn this is how to handle big emotions. Like many values and skills we try to teach our kids, emotional regulation skills are more often "caught" than "taught." The skills and principles we talk about in this chapter can just as easily apply to our own lives as we work toward being a good example for our children.

EMOTIONAL REGULATION IN INFANTS

The most effective strategies to help kids with emotional regulation vary by age.[1] This probably is not surprising, but infants have limited abilities to regulate their emotions. For infants, cries are generally an attempt to avoid unpleasant stimuli or approach pleasant stimuli, such as food or touch.[2] Infants need us to help them soothe and regulate their emotions—they can't do it themselves. We need to be their co-regulators. The best thing to do with an infant is respond calmly to their emotions and work to meet their need (comfort, food, diaper change, sleep) as best you can. Music and singing can also help with emotional regulation in infants.[3] Finally, infants can engage in self-soothing behavior such as sucking.[4] Some parents discourage infants from sucking their thumb or using a pacifier because they worry it could become a habit that will later be difficult to break, but if your infant has found a strategy to self-soothe, it can be helpful to let them do it. At this early stage, it's age appropriate. They are working on developing emotional regulation skills in the only way they know how.

EMOTIONAL REGULATION IN TODDLERS

Children's abilities to regulate their emotions increase with age, but younger toddlers are still quite limited in their abilities to control their emotions. Parents sometimes set expectations too high for very young children, expecting them to act like an older child. For most young toddlers, this is simply not possible. Plus, trauma experiences can impair a child's brain, causing them to function at about half their developmental age. Their brains are not developed enough to engage in sophisticated strategies to control their emotional expressions. Similar to infants, they have an emotion and it comes out how it comes out.

Young toddlers, then, still need us to help them soothe and manage their emotions. Holding and rocking a toddler, for example, and talking softly or singing to them can help them calm down. Be calm yourself, and engage your toddler calmly. For younger toddlers, doing something to change the situation, removing them from the stimulus that is upsetting them, or distracting them with a toy or new activity can also help with emotional regulation.[5] This may look like going outside, letting warm water run over their hands, or getting a snack. Remember, toddlers are going through big developmental changes. Feelings can be overwhelming as they learn to develop coping strategies, especially when they have a trauma history. Many parents make the mistake of ignoring the undesired behavior in their child for fear they are enabling the behavior or because they believe their child is manipulating them. This is not true. You are not enabling the behavior and your child's brain is not capable of manipulation at this age. Your child is communicating a need. Instead, a better strategy is to model regulation skills and be your child's co-regulator. Remember, you are responding to a trauma history in your child, which means you need to help disarm the child's fear response by connecting with them, not ignoring or pushing them away.

EMOTIONAL REGULATION IN OLDER CHILDREN

With older children, you can begin to teach them more sophisticated strategies for understanding and managing their emotions. Remember, learning emotional regulation skills is a process—it doesn't happen overnight. When teaching emotional regulation skills, try thinking about this process in three steps: (1) learning about emotions, (2) understanding what activates strong emotions, and (3) identifying appropriate ways to respond to emotions.[6] And honestly, these strategies can be helpful for our own big feelings as well.

Learning about emotions

Managing an emotion is difficult if you can't identify and talk about your feelings. It is helpful for families to have a shared language about emotions. For example, one acronym I use to help identify emotions is SASHET—sad, angry, scared, happy, excited, and tender.[7] A simpler rhyme I sometimes use with kids is "sad, glad, mad, and a-frad" (referring to "afraid"). For even younger kids, try feeling charts with faces that display different emotions and their names.

Whatever strategy you use, it's important to make emotions—both your emotions and those you observe throughout the day—something you regularly talk and learn about with your kids. For example, if you see someone yelling outside or on the television, you could say something like "Boy, he sure feels mad." When you share your own feelings, be sure to give a brief context so your child starts to connect feelings to their causes—for example, "I feel excited because we are going on vacation to see Nana and Papa tomorrow." Model your feelings to your child. This can be hard to do if you're used to stuffing your feelings down or internalizing them. But by modeling your feelings, you are helping your child understand that all their feelings are a normal part of what it means to be human. Feelings aren't good or bad—they just are what they are. So model all of them.

Understanding what activates strong emotions

Once you help kids develop language to identify and talk about their emotions, you can work with them to understand what triggers their emotions. Continuing to share about the emotions you experience, and the context around them, can help model this for your children. But you can also be proactive in helping your kids learn to connect these dots themselves. For example, when your child experiences a strong emotion, ask them to slow down and think about the following questions:

- *What happened?* What was the situation that made them feel this way?
- *How do you feel?* Using the framework you have taught your child, ask them what emotion they are experiencing. For example, are they feeling sad, glad, mad, or a-frad?
- *How strong is the feeling?* It can be helpful to teach kids that emotions can vary in intensity, and the intensity of their emotional experience can increase or decrease over time. An easy way to do this is have them rate the intensity of their emotion from one to ten.
- *Do you feel anything in your body?* When we have a feeling, we often experience something physical in our body. For example, if we are feeling sad, we might feel heaviness in our chest. If we are feeling scared, we might feel butterflies in our stomach. If we are feeling mad, we might feel tense and have rapid breathing. If you can teach kids to link their bodily sensations with different emotions, it can help them understand what they are feeling.
- *What did you do?* How did you respond? If you could go back and do it over, would you respond in the same way, or do something different?

For a child who is completely dysregulated, it will be impossible to respond to these questions in the moment. The goal would be to help them return to a calm baseline before having a conversation. But for kids who are experiencing big emotions but are relatively calm, you could engage them in the questions above. (Older kids who are struggling to manage their emotions could keep a journal and record answers to these questions whenever they experience a strong emotion.)

Identifying appropriate ways to respond to emotions
Once children can talk about their emotions and understand the contexts in which they arise, the final step is to help them identify appropriate ways to respond to or manage their emotions. This is what we refer to as coping strategies—things they can learn to do to manage a big emotion in an age-appropriate manner.

When working with coping strategies, there are a few organizing principles to keep in mind. First, it's good to have a variety of coping strategies—the more the better. Some coping strategies will work better for certain kids than others, and some coping strategies may work better in some situations than others. Try to give your kids several options, and see what works best for them. Second, for the most part, certain coping strategies aren't better or worse than other coping strategies. If a coping strategy is safe and seems to work for your child, go ahead and add it to the repertoire. Third, having coping strategies close at hand and easy to access will help children remember to engage the strategies when they need them. One idea is to write down or print an image of coping strategy ideas on a big poster board and put it somewhere where your child can easily see it. Another idea is to give your child a card they can put in their pocket with ideas for coping strategies written on it. Or you could use a "calm down" jar. In the jar, put pieces of paper with coping strategy ideas for your child to try. When they need one, they can reach in the jar and try whatever is on the paper. The key is practice. You need your child to practice coping skills when they are calm and regulated. Then they can access them more easily because of muscle memory when they need them the most.

If you are having trouble coming up with coping strategies to teach your child, here are some ideas to get you started.[8]

- Activities that are visually calming (sand timer, fish tank, indoor fountain)
- Activities to help unwind (blow bubbles as big as you can, which mimics taking a deep breath; blow up a balloon; color; read; listen to music)
- Comforting activities (warm bath, hugs)
- Activities that focus attention on other things (painting, connect-the-dot pictures, meditation)
- Physical activities that release tension (trampoline jumping, wall pushes, seat pulls)
- Things to hold or squeeze (stress balls, slime, fidget spinners)
- Activities that engage the mouth (chewing gum, sucking through a twisty straw)

THE IMPORTANCE OF REHEARSAL

I'll say it again: It is essential to talk about emotions and practice different coping skills *before* the child needs to use them. If you practice coping strategies in calm situations, they will become a habit, and your child will be more likely to engage these coping strategies when they really need them.

Here are a couple of suggestions to help with rehearsal and practice. One exercise I like to do with kids is called "How's your engine running?" You can draw a picture showing a fuel gauge where blue indicates low energy, green indicates medium energy, and red indicates high energy. Discuss that there are times when our engine should be in the red, such as gym class. And there are times when our engine should be in the blue, such as before bed. But sometimes our engines run out of sync with the situation, and when they do, we can use our coping skills to get back to the green zone. You can ask children to pause and check in with themselves to see how their engine is running. If the engine is running close to red (too high), it might be time to do something to try to calm down.

Another suggestion for practice and rehearsal is to have your kids do something to *intentionally* dysregulate their bodies—for example, do jumping jacks for twenty seconds as fast as they can. Check in with your child and ask them to identify what they are feeling in their body. Are they breathing heavy, is their heart pounding, or do they feel sweaty? Do the physical symptoms they are experiencing feel similar to any emotions they experience, like anger? This develops great body awareness. Then, when their body is dysregulated, they can practice their coping strategies to try to calm down and get back to the green zone from the "How's your engine running?" activity. In this way, they simulate an experience of dysregulation and can experience how it feels to engage in a coping strategy when their body is revved up.

DONALD AND AVERY

Let's go back to the example of Donald and Avery from the beginning of this chapter. Avery struggled to manage his emotions when they went to the grocery store and Donald gave him the limit of choosing only one item to buy. Avery had a meltdown, and they had to leave the grocery store immediately. What could Donald have done to improve their chances for a successful grocery store trip?

Before we move forward in this example, I want to point out that emotional regulation doesn't always work, even if we do our best to teach our kids well and give them ample coping strategies to try. Emotional regulation is not easy. It's not always easy for us as adults, and it certainly isn't easy for kids who are just learning these skills. Donald may try to do everything right, and his son may still melt down in the grocery store aisle. That said, let's consider this conversation between Donald and Avery as they prepare for another trip to the store.

DONALD. Hey, buddy, before we go to the store, I'd like to talk about something.

AVERY. Sure, Daddy. What?

DONALD. Well, last time we went to the store, you had some big feelings. Do you remember?

AVERY. Yeah . . .

DONALD. What were you feeling? [*points to the feeling chart on the refrigerator*] Was it glad, sad, mad, or a-frad?

AVERY. I guess mad.

DONALD. Yeah, that was my guess too. Now, when we go to the store this time, do you think you might feel mad again?

AVERY. I hope not, but maybe.

DONALD. Yeah, well, it's okay to feel mad sometimes. We all feel that way sometimes. But the important thing is what we do with it. Now, I'm wondering, what could you do this time if you feel mad?

AVERY. I guess I could squeeze my ball.

DONALD. Yeah, you could squeeze your ball. That's a good idea. Why don't we practice that right now? What about this? I'd like you to pretend to be mad—what would you do if you were mad?

AVERY. I'd yell and stomp my foot.

DONALD. Yeah, so you would yell and stomp your foot. So let's practice yelling and stomping your feet. Then let's practice squeezing our ball.

AVERY. [*smiles*] You want me to practice yelling? I can do that!

DONALD. Ha ha, I know, buddy.

What principles or strategies from the chapter do you see modeled in this example?

DISCUSSION QUESTIONS

- What stuck out to you most as you read this chapter? What did you learn about emotional regulation that you didn't know previously?
- How are you doing at modeling emotional regulation skills for your children? Do you talk about emotions regularly? Do you share how you are feeling and the context for your emotions? Do you model healthy coping skills for your kids?
- What is one strategy you could implement today to help your kids identify, understand, and manage their emotions?

15

HELPING CHILDREN FIND THEIR VOICE

An important part of growing up is finding our voice—becoming our own person, complete with our own personality, thoughts, feelings, wants, questions, and story. But we can't do this alone. We need the people around us—especially our parents and caretakers—to nurture this in us, to support us in this process. For many children who have been adopted or have spent time in foster care, this hasn't been the case. Often, hard decisions have been made for them, and their parents or caretakers who struggled to meet their basic needs may have also struggled to foster their individuality and voice. Their trauma history compounds the challenges they face in finding their voice. So how can we help them do so?

MARIO

Fourteen-year-old Mario is currently in foster care. When I met Mario, the first thing I noticed was how small and quiet he seemed. He was unassuming—if you weren't focused on connecting with him, you might even forget he was there. He tended to blend into the background and remain unseen. If you asked him a question or his opinion on something, he would generally shrug his shoulders, as if to say, "I don't know." He hadn't discovered his own voice.

When I learned more about Mario's story, some of his behaviors started to make sense. Mario was abused and neglected as a child. By the time I met him, he had spent several years in foster care. Most of the decisions that determined the trajectory of his life—being removed from his birth parents, being placed in a foster home, changing placements, not being able to reunify with his birth parents—were made for him by others in authority, without his consent. (Sometimes this is necessary—many of these decisions were made for Mario's safety. Still, some of these decisions can have unintended consequences: children can struggle to find their voice when it hasn't seemed to matter in big decisions about their own lives.) Mario had questions about his past, his story, and his future—and many of these questions remained unanswered. Sometimes this was because his foster parents didn't know the answers, and sometimes this was because they felt that answering a question would cause Mario more pain (such as telling him that his birth father was in jail). A lot was going on with Mario, but I knew at least part of our work together would focus on helping him find his voice.

STRUGGLING TO FIND YOUR VOICE

When a child is growing up, an important part of their development is feeling supported in their independence and autonomy in age-appropriate ways. As parents, we want to encourage children to explore, try things out, and find their sense of self. But sometimes things happen along the way that make this process more difficult—especially for kids who have been adopted or spent time in foster care.

When children are the victims of abuse or neglect, finding their voice and sense of self is difficult. Remember our discussion of Maslow's hierarchy of needs in chapter 11? Feeling safe and secure in one's environment is a foundational need. Children cannot feel comfortable exploring their environment and trying new things on their own until this need has been met. If safety and security were not in place early on for a child, the development of their autonomous self may be stunted. Trauma stifles a child's voice. Children who have been hurt soon realize their voice doesn't matter and that the only person they can trust is themselves.

Children who are adopted or have spent time in foster care often have big decisions made for them—and they may have had little or no say in these decisions. For example, children often don't have much say about whether an adoption plan is created, or whether they will reunite with their birth family. Children in foster care don't usually have a say in placement decisions, or how long they will stay. These decisions affect their life tremendously, and it makes sense that they would want to decide themselves, or at least have a vote. But this usually isn't possible.

Children often have a lot of questions about their situation, their history, and their future. Asking questions and getting answers can help children feel empowered and find their voice, but unfortunately, their biggest questions often go unanswered. Sometimes this is because parents and other people in the system don't know the answers. And sometimes this is because parents and other people in the system want to protect the child from pain.

HELPING CHILDREN FIND THEIR VOICE
When our children struggle to find their voice, what can we do to help them find it? Here a few helpful practices to try:

Provide space for feelings

Throughout this book, I have talked about the importance of working with children and their feelings. Perhaps unsurprisingly, consistently providing a space for children to share their feelings is a great way to begin to help them find their voice. Being able to identify what they are feeling, share what they are feeling, and be affirmed for what they are feeling enables kids to connect with themselves in a deeper way. It is important for us as parents to press pause on our own feelings or reactions to give permission for our child's experience. (We can get back to our feelings later.) For example, would you feel triggered if your child were to say, "I wonder what my life would've been like if my mom didn't make an adoption plan and I got to live with her"? Would it be safe for your child to express that to you? Look, I get it. This is tough stuff. Yet it is so important to create a safe place for our child to explore all their feelings without negatively influencing their story. We have already talked about some foundational ways to help kids get in touch with their feelings, such as teaching kids a framework for talking about feelings (e.g., mad, sad, glad, a-frad) and modeling via sharing your own feelings. Here are a few more ideas:

One idea is to have a daily family check-in. It doesn't have to take a long time, but intentionally set aside a few minutes each day where family members can check in with how they are feeling. Have each family member pick one feeling they experienced that day and give a brief (one- to two-minute) context around that feeling. For example, you could go first and say, "I feel angry because one of my coworkers was rude to me at work." In a similar way, some families have a daily time of sharing where they each say a "rose" and a "thorn" (something good and something tough) for that day. Depending on the size of your family, this whole exercise could take five to ten minutes. But if you do it every day, it will help your family get in the habit of getting in touch with and talking about their feelings.

Therapist and author Paris Goodyear-Brown recommends the practice of drawing a "feelings heart."[1] First, have the child draw a big heart on a piece of paper. Then have the child pick a few feelings and assign each of them a color ("What color goes with happy? What color goes with sad?"). Then pick a couple of feelings yourself and have your child assign them a color as well. (Children sometimes focus only on the "positive" emotions, so I recommend parents pick a couple of feelings in order to include a range of emotions.) Then have your child color in the heart with different colors according to how they are feeling right now. You can then ask them about the parts of their heart ("Can you tell me about your heart? Can you tell me about the happy part of your heart? Can you tell me about the sad part of your heart?").

One final activity I have used in counseling is to play "feelings Candy Land." As you set up the Candy Land game board, assign one feeling to each color. Each time you flip a card while playing the game, share a time when you experienced that feeling ("I feel angry when my brother takes my toy"; "I feel happy when I get to play soccer"). You can also recall a time in your past when you felt that feeling ("I felt sad when my friend was diagnosed with cancer"). Take a turn and then have your child take a turn. This activity can help your child learn to express feelings in a light, playful context, and shows your child you have feelings, too, and that all feelings are okay.

Listen well

It's not enough to simply provide space for our children to share their feelings—we must also listen well. For most of us, listening well can be difficult. We might get distracted when our child is talking, or think about how to respond next. How can we truly listen well so our children feel loved and cared for? Here are a few suggestions:

When you are with your child, try to remove all distractions that might take your attention away from listening. For example, turn off the television, put away your phone, and shut down the computer. I have heard of some families who have a "phone box" where all family members place their phones when they are at home. I think this is a great idea to help keep families engaged with each other.

It can be helpful to think about how we can listen with our body and posture. One acronym to help you listen well is SOLER:

- Face your child *squarely* when you listen
- Have an *open* body posture
- *Lean* forward rather than away
- Make *eye* contact with your child
- Be *relaxed* rather than tense[2]

Another helpful strategy is to paraphrase or mirror what your child says. For example, when your child shares something, say something like "What I hear you saying is [paraphrase what your child has said]." Paraphrasing helps your child know you are listening to them and tracking what they are saying. They can also correct you if you didn't get it quite right, which can help reduce misunderstandings.

It can also be helpful to empathize and validate what your child is saying. Empathizing is similar to paraphrasing but reflects back the feelings your child is sharing. For example, you could say something like "It sounds like you are feeling sad about what happened at school." Validation involves letting your child know that you affirm them and that what they shared makes sense to you. Again, you could respond to your child by saying, "I think it makes a lot of sense that you would feel mad at Joey for talking behind your back. I would feel the same way if I were in your situation." Validating your child's emotions can be a game changer.

Encourage questions

Anyone who has spent time with a child between the ages of two and ten has probably heard the word *why* more than any other. Children ask lots of questions. Children who are adopted or in foster care are the same way. Sometimes, however, because of their history and experiences, their questions can be tougher. In general, it's good to answer a child's questions in an age-appropriate way to the best of your ability. Answering questions helps a child understand who they are in a deeper way and ultimately helps them find their voice.

But answering our children's questions is sometimes easier said than done. They might ask questions we do not know the answer to ("How long will I be here before I can go back to live with my birth family?"). Or they might ask questions that we know the answer to, but we worry it will be painful for them to hear it (such as their birth parents' parental rights were terminated). Or we might know the answer but not know how to communicate it in an age-appropriate way (for example, their birth father was arrested and is currently in jail for rape). These are tricky situations, and there are often no easy answers.

One strategy I have used with parents who find themselves facing difficult questions from their children is to create a question book where children can write all the questions they have about themselves, their birth family, and other parts of their history. If a parent doesn't know the answer to a question or doesn't know how to answer the question in an age-appropriate way, the child can write it down in their question book. This practice communicates to the child that their questions are valid and that you will try to get an answer if possible. This also gives parents time to either try to find the answer to the question or consult with a professional about how to answer the question in an age-appropriate manner.

Another exercise I have used with children is to encourage them to write a letter asking all the questions they wonder about. For example, a child might write a letter to their birth parent, expressing all their questions, curiosities, and feelings. They might say things like "I wish I could meet you," "I wonder if you look like me," or "Why did you abandon me?" Don't send the letter, but use it as a jumping-off point for discussing the questions your child has. (Make sure you are clear with your child ahead of time that you will not be sending the letter and you will read it.) You may be able to find answers to some of the questions, but some might be impossible to answer. The point is to have your child get all their questions down on paper so you can process and talk about them together.

We often think more along the lines of "protecting our children from" rather than "helping our children through." But if we want to help our children find their voice, we must honor all their questions and curiosities, even if this leads to more confusion or difficult feelings. This is their life, and they have the right to know. Sometimes we might think that answering certain questions would cause more pain for our children. But our children already have the questions. If we don't help them find answers, they will try to find the answers by themselves. It is better to be in relationship with our children and help them find the answers than to leave them alone with their questions. This helps develop trust between you.

Learn about their story

We will talk in more detail about honoring all parts of a child's story in the next chapter. But briefly, helping kids learn about their story can be an important way to help them find their voice. Most of us get a sense of rootedness from our family of origin. This shared history helps us know where we come from. Some children who are adopted or in foster care may not have as much connection with their biological family history, and this loss can contribute to their struggle in finding their voice.

As much as possible, try to help your child learn about their story. Keep or find as many records as you can, including mementos, souvenirs, pictures from orphanages or placements, and medical records. Gather as much information as you can about your child's story and where they came from. You might seek out multiple sources, including the adoption or foster care agency, caseworkers who have been involved with your child, and members of your child's birth family. If your child wants to find or connect with their birth family, help them with this process (assuming it is safe to do so). If your child wants to connect with their cultural background or visit their country or region of birth, support them in this endeavor as much as you can. This can help fill in the gaps when your child is curious about their history.

One exercise I have found useful when helping kids learn about their story is to keep a "story box." We create a special box where they can keep all their important things. It could be as simple as a cardboard box, or you could purchase a wooden box and your child could decorate it. But in that box, the child

can store all the things about their history that are meaningful to them. This could include records, pictures, souvenirs,
or other items from their birth family or country of origin.
Then you can look through the box and talk about the items
together, which can help them reconnect with their history.

Counseling

I have mentioned counseling as an option several times
throughout this book, and it bears repeating in this chapter. One of the best ways to help children find their voice is
individual counseling with a trauma-informed therapist. In
normal day-to-day life, it can be challenging to give our kids
long periods of undivided attention where we really listen
and tune in to how they are doing and what they would like
to say. We try our best, but we are often balancing so many
responsibilities and other priorities that these long periods of
undivided attention are difficult to come by. And even if we are
able to give our child this undivided attention, we don't have
the training and expertise that a professional offers. Therapy
can be a great addition to the parenting work you are already
doing with your kids. In therapy, your child will get to spend
consistent, one-on-one time with a trained counselor who
can help them in numerous ways—to understand their story,
work through their questions, and make peace with their past,
among other areas of focus. Even if your child doesn't have
something specific that they want to address in counseling, a
counselor can help them process issues related to family, adoption, and foster care.

Some Christians may feel that psychology and mental
health counseling could run counter to having faith in God.
For example, I have talked with parents who wanted spiritual
support for their children instead of mental health support.

Although I think prayer and spiritual support is great, it does not replace the effectiveness of working with a licensed mental health professional. Both are important. If your child broke a leg, you would never only pray for their healing. You may pray as part of a larger effort to help, but you would also take them to a doctor trained in orthopedics. In the same way, it's important to find a trained mental health specialist who can support your child. When in doubt, get more help.

MARIO

Check out this dialogue between Mario, whom we met earlier in this chapter, and his foster mom Carol as she introduces the idea of a story box.

> CAROL. Hi, Mario, I noticed you have some items from your birth family in your bag. Would you like to show them to me?
>
> MARIO. Yeah, I guess.
>
> CAROL. Okay, why don't you pick one and tell me about it?
>
> MARIO. [*pulls out a small plastic baseball helmet*] I didn't get to see my dad much after I got put in foster care, but on one of the visits, we went to get ice cream and you could get your ice cream in one of these baseball helmets. So I kept that.
>
> CAROL. It sounds like you really treasure that memory of your dad.
>
> MARIO. Yeah, I guess so. I wish I could see him.
>
> CAROL. It sounds like you really miss him. What is something else you have in your bag?

MARIO. [*pulls out a trophy*] This was my soccer trophy from when I was younger. I was pretty good and even scored a few goals that season.

CAROL. Do you like playing soccer?

MARIO. Well, I don't really play much anymore. But I guess I used to like it.

CAROL. Okay, what else do you have in your bag?

MARIO. [*pulls out a small photograph*] This is a picture of me and my parents.

CAROL. Thanks for sharing that with me. What feelings come up when you look at that picture? [*points to the feeling chart*]

MARIO. I guess sad. We look happy in the picture, but we weren't really that happy most of the time.

CAROL. Yeah, that makes sense. We've talked about some tough stuff that happened when you were growing up, and it seems a bit different from the smiles in the picture.

MARIO. Yeah.

CAROL. I want to thank you for showing these things to me, Mario. Even though these don't always bring up happy memories, it can be good to remember our stories, and items like these can help us. Sometimes kids find it helpful to put them all in a special place—I call this a "story box." What do you think of that?

MARIO. Yeah, it's probably better than this old bag.

What principles from this chapter on helping kids find their voice do you notice in this dialogue between Mario and his foster mom?

DISCUSSION QUESTIONS

- What stood out to you most as you read this chapter? What did you learn about helping your children find their voice that you didn't know previously?

- How are you doing at providing space for your children's feelings? What feelings are most challenging for you to hold?

- How are you doing at providing space for your children's questions and helping them find answers as much as possible? What questions are most difficult for you to handle?

16

HONORING A
CHILD'S STORY

In the previous chapter, we took a deep dive into helping children find their voice. Part of that process involved helping them learn about their story. Children who are adopted or have spent time in foster care often struggle with their story, either because it involves a lot of pain, such as trauma experiences or being unable to reunite with their birth family, or because parts of it are unknown, such as who their birth dad is, or certain gaps in history, or details from the orphanage. Helping children connect with and own their story can contribute to a stronger sense of self and identity.

But honoring a child's developing story isn't always easy. How do we talk with our children about their story? How do we honor a child's interpretation of their developing story, even if we disagree or see things differently? And what do we do with the unknowns or gaps in a child's story? If you have ever struggled to engage with your child about their story, my hope is this chapter will offer some thoughts and a framework for how to do that.

BRAD, DEB, AND CRAIG

Brad and Deb Taylor adopted Craig when he was eight years old. They had two older biological children—Patrick (age fourteen) and Dennis (age eleven). Craig had been put in foster care when he was five years old because his biological mother had consistent struggles with drug use and legal problems. His biological dad was unknown. Craig bounced around at a couple of foster care placements before landing with the Taylors. Eventually, his birth mother's parental rights were terminated, and the Taylors adopted Craig.

One of the challenges Brad and Deb faced was helping Craig learn about his developing story. Early on, it was challenging to even explain the basics of adoption to Craig—Craig wanted to go back to his birth mother and didn't understand why he couldn't. Brad and Deb weren't sure how to communicate to Craig the facts of his situation. He had a very positive view of his birth mother—and Brad and Deb struggled with whether they should tell him more about her situation (that she had a history of drug abuse and had spent time in jail, and it was likely that her parental rights would be terminated). Craig also was curious about his biological dad. They tried to help Craig get more information about his bio dad, but were unsuccessful—Craig's birth mom didn't know who he was. These conversations (or the lack of conversations) put a strain on the relationship between Craig and his adoptive parents. As Craig grew older, Brad and Deb knew he needed to hear more about his story, but they didn't know how to talk about this respectfully.

THE IMPORTANCE OF KNOWING YOUR STORY

As we've already discussed, children need to know the fullness of their story—even the difficult or painful aspects. Many parents think they are protecting their children by holding back or not sharing certain aspects of their child's story, but this is usually not helpful. Instead of trying to protect your child from their story, be honest with them—as is developmentally appropriate—and then support them with whatever comes up. Some children will be curious about their story, and other children will be uninterested. It's okay to follow your child's lead, but at minimum, communicate the details and let your child know the topic is always open for conversation. Next, we'll look at why and how we can do this.

HOW TO TALK WITH CHILDREN ABOUT THEIR STORY

What does it look like to talk with your child about their story in a developmentally appropriate way? First, let's go over some principles for talking with younger children, and then we'll move to some principles for talking with older children.

Talking with younger kids (ages zero to seven)

Even if a child is very small, it is important to be honest with them about their story from day one. Some parents choose not to tell a child that they are adopted or in foster care, which can cause problems when they eventually find out at an older age. If they find this out at an older age, they may be angry or feel deceived, which can damage your relationship. This is an important part of your child's story, and it's important to tell them starting right away. Let them know that they are adopted or in foster care from day one.

If you have very young kids, it can be hard to explain adoption or foster care. Sometimes it is helpful to use dolls or pictures. You can explain that their birth mom and dad are the ones who gave birth to them. But sometimes kids have other parents who take care of them. You can also explain that sometimes parents can look different from the child, which is an important point if you have a transracial family. When talking about adoption or foster care, be cognizant of the language you use. To look at a common phrase, instead of saying "Your birth mom and dad 'gave you up' for adoption," say "They made an adoption plan." Use respectful language as much as possible.

When you tell younger kids they are adopted or in foster care, it may bring up some fear or uncertainty about their place in the family. Be sure to reassure your child they are part of the family and you love them no matter what. If the placement is permanent, let them know that as well ("You will be part of our family forever") so they don't worry about not being able to stay with you long-term.

Talking with older kids (ages eight to twelve—and above)

As children grow up, you can begin to tell them more about their story, including the difficult or painful aspects. There's no hard-and-fast rule about what you should reveal and when, but one rule of thumb is that by the time your child is twelve, they should know *all* the details—share with them everything you know about their story. At this age, your child can handle even the difficult and painful aspects of their story. Younger children tend to focus on the happy parts of adoption, but around second or third grade, children begin to understand cognitively that for adoption to happen, their birth family had to relinquish their rights. This can bring up a range of feelings, and you want to support your child in this process. Also, during the teenage years, children often want to separate from their parents and rely more on their friends for support. By telling your child the fullness of their story before they become a teenager, it gives them time to process their story with you while you have a close bond.

Even when the details of their story are uncomfortable or heavy, it is good to tell children their full story as you know it. If you hold things back or omit facts about their history, they may feel betrayed by you when they grow up and learn the truth about their past themselves. Plus, as children grow up, their understanding about their family, where they came from, and how it affects them will evolve with them. Don't shy away from sharing all the details.

Being honest and forthcoming with children about their story builds trust between you, which is one of the key parts of effective parenting. That trust will enable them to come to you with their problems and struggles down the road and lean on you for help and support. When you talk with older children about their story, make space for all their feelings and reactions. Feelings such as grief, loss, and anger are all normal and okay—it doesn't mean you did something wrong by sharing or that you shouldn't have shared. Older kids often begin to search out information about their past or history on their own, and ideally you want to be a partner in this process rather than a brake-pusher. It's better for them to hear the facts of their story from you than from the internet or a third party.

When adoptive or foster parents hear that a child wants more information about their birth family, or wants to seek out their birth family, it can feel threatening—like they aren't "enough." Most children are curious about their birth families, and their birth families will always be a part of their story. There is enough room for kids to hold space for both sets of parents in their hearts—if a child wants to seek out their birth family, it doesn't mean they don't love you or don't want a relationship with you.

It is also normal for a child who is adopted or in foster care to (at some point) use the term "real" mom or "real" dad when referencing their birth family. For example, "Why did my real mom give me up?" Your child may have even yelled this at you—"You're not my real dad!" It's important to not get defensive when this happens, even though it might sting. Your child is developing language around their story. Recalling some of the strategies we've shared, you could respond in the following way: "Well, I feel pretty real." (Remember: playfulness disarms fear.) "But I know when you say 'real' you mean your birth dad." (Paraphrase and reflect back what you heard.) "And you're right, I'm not your birth dad, but I am your dad and I love you very much. It's okay to have all your feelings about this." (Provide validation.) "I wonder whether you're having some feelings about your adoption story."

If you do find yourself reacting or getting defensive, it may be helpful to see a counselor and sort out some of these feelings and reactions so they don't harm your relationship with your child.

HONORING YOUR CHILD'S INTERPRETATION OF THEIR STORY

A common challenge for parents is what to do when your child's interpretation of their story does not line up with your interpretation of their story. This can be particularly difficult when it relates to your child's opinion of their birth parents, or the adoption process in general. For example, your child might think their birth parents are amazing and put them up on a pedestal, but you know they physically abused your child before the child came into your care, or they have legal problems or are misusing drugs. What should you do when there is a mismatch between how you and your children understand their story?

When we approach differences of opinion, our natural tendency is to assert our position or try to convince the other person we are correct. Sometimes we do this by villainizing the birth parents so our child will align with our view. When it comes to your children and their story, however, this strategy usually isn't effective. Everyone's perspective is different. Our perspectives and stories are partly based on the facts, but we also bring our histories and motivations to the table when we construct our stories. Because you and your child have different histories and motivations, it isn't surprising that your stories or interpretations may be different.

If your story or interpretation is different from your child's, the best thing to do is mirror and validate their feelings. Do not try to change their view of their story or their birth family. Continuing the example above, when you hear your child's story about their birth parents, you might respond by saying something like "I hear you really love your birth family and miss them." This gets to the heart of what your child is trying to communicate to you. This is a better strategy than trying to argue with your child or assert your position—doing this will only create a division between you.

Children's thoughts and feelings toward their birth parents (and toward their adoptive and foster parents) are likely to shift and change over time. Instead of arguing or feeling threatened by your child's story right now, give them some space and let it play out. Your child is constructing a story about their history and how their life is progressing, and this takes time and evolves over time. Let them develop their own story—don't force your interpretation onto their narrative.

DEALING WITH UNKNOWNS

When you begin to engage with your child around their story, you will almost certainly run into some unknowns. Your child may not know their birth parents, or even who their birth parents are. They might not know if they spent time in an orphanage, or what that experience was like. They might not know why they were adopted or placed in foster care. They might not know the details of their medical history, or whether they were abused or neglected.

Unknowns can be scary. It helps us feel a sense of safety and security when we know our story and history. This drives some children to seek out the answers to their unknowns and fill in the blanks in their story. As much as possible, help your children with this process. Help them find the answers to their questions. Partner with them in this quest. For example, check in with the adoption agency, or go back and visit the orphanage and their country of origin. Help them connect to those missing pieces of who they are as much as possible.

Even if you try your best to help kids get answers to their questions, there may still be some unknowns. If that happens, empathize with your child if you don't know or can't find the answer to their question. Understand that not being able to find these answers is often a loss for them. Grieve with them if important questions go unanswered. Give space for all their feelings—don't rush them through this process. This is another point when having a counselor can be helpful—to give kids a space to process everything that comes up for them.

BRAD, DEB, AND CRAIG

Brad and Deb, whom we met earlier in this chapter, were challenged to talk with Craig in a developmentally appropriate manner about adoption and some of the struggles that his birth mom was going through. Check out this dialogue between Brad and Deb and eight-year-old Craig when they found out his birth mom's parental rights were being terminated and they were going to adopt him.

BRAD. Hey, can we talk to you for a minute?

CRAIG. Yeah.

BRAD. Well, it's about your birth mom. We heard from the judge that she isn't going to be able to take you back. I know this isn't what you were hoping for, and that you love her very much. She loves you, too—it's just that she continues to have some problems and isn't able to provide a safe home for you.

CRAIG. [*doesn't say anything—just looks at the floor*]

DEB. We also want you to know that the judge said you can stay with us—that we can adopt you.

CRAIG. So I just have to wait a little longer to go home then?

BRAD. Well, I know this is hard, buddy, but because your mom isn't able to take care of you, you're going to stay here with us while you grow up, as part of our family. We will still be able to visit your birth mom, so you will be able to see her. But you won't be able to go live with her.

CRAIG. [*continues looking at the floor*]

DEB. I know this is so hard and not what you were hoping for. But I want you to know we love you very much and will do our best to love and care for you—and help you stay connected to your birth mom as best we can.

BRAD. And if you want to talk about anything, we're here. It's okay to have all your feelings. I imagine you might be feeling disappointed, sad, and maybe even a little angry.

CRAIG. Yeah, okay.

BRAD. What if we draw a heart and draw all the feelings we are feeling in the heart? I'll do one too.

CRAIG. Okay.

What do you think about how Brad and Deb talked with Craig about this very difficult issue? Is there anything you would adjust or change if you were to have this conversation with your child?

DISCUSSION QUESTIONS

- What stuck out to you most as you read this chapter? What did you learn about engaging with your child's story that you didn't know previously?
- What is challenging about or holds you back from fully engaging with your child about their story?
- How are you doing at engaging with your child about the missing pieces or unknowns about their story?

17

NAVIGATING RELATIONSHIPS WITH BIRTH FAMILIES

One of the more challenging aspects of adoptive and foster parenting is navigating your family's relationship with your child's birth family. This is a tough topic. It often brings up strong feelings and reactions in adoptive and foster parents, and we will discuss some of these reactions in this chapter. Also, real safety issues can sometimes make certain boundaries necessary when navigating this relationship. Always prioritize the safety of your child.

With those caveats, I do believe it is a good idea, when possible, to do as much as you can to have a good relationship with your child's birth parents and include them in the life of your child and family. That said, it's important to follow your child's lead. There may be times when they may want more contact or less. And the type of relationship you have with the birth parents also depends on their willingness to be in relationship with you.

When I was a therapist for kids in the foster care system, I also worked with many birth families who were working hard to get their kids back. Many of these birth parents came from very challenging backgrounds and were in very difficult situations. They were working incredibly hard and showing a lot of courage trying to do what they needed to do to get their kids back. Some of the birth parents I worked with felt supported by the system and the foster parents who were caring for their kids, but many did not. Many felt villainized by the system and foster parents, and this broke my heart. I so badly wanted all of us to be on the same side, doing everything we could to help preserve the family.

I truly believe God wants all of us to experience healing, including birth parents whose children are in foster care. And I also believe that no person is beyond the redemptive healing of Jesus. He loves each of us deeply and is capable of transforming all lives, including the lives of birth parents. I think Jesus would be cheering for and supporting birth parents to experience healing (regardless of the outcome), and I want to be someone who models the same. I love how author and foster mom Jamie Finn puts it: "I want eyes that see my kids' parents as my God sees them. I want a heart that loves them as He loves them."[1]

Your relationship with the birth family will depend on your context. If you are a foster family, visits (usually weekly) will be mandated and set up by the foster care agency and your caseworker. The frequency and length of the visits will be set for you, but there is still some flexibility about how you engage with the birth parents. If you are an adoptive family and the parental rights of the birth family have been terminated, there is more flexibility for you to decide how to engage with the birth parents and family. The adoption plan may have certain guidelines (e.g., open or closed), which will help direct the contact with the birth family early on. However, open adoptions take many forms, and even in closed adoptions, your child may want to seek out their birth parents as they grow older. In this chapter, we'll cover some helpful principles for relationships with birth parents, but be sure to adapt these suggestions to your context.

DOUG AND ELISSA

Doug and Elissa married in their mid-twenties, and like many people who get involved with foster care, they had hearts for caring for children in need. Doug was a pastor and Elissa was a teacher who decided to stay at home when they had their first biological child, a girl named Parker. Two years later, they had a biological son named Grant. When Parker was five and Grant was three, Doug and Elissa applied to become foster parents and got licensed.

Their first placement was a one-year-old boy named David. Doug and Elissa fell in love with David right away. David had been neglected by his biological mother and physically abused by some members of his biological extended family and had some developmental delays. Doug and Elissa were determined to give David all the love and support they could. They were all in.

One aspect of foster parenting they were not necessarily prepared for was navigating the relationship with David's birth parents. David's bio dad wasn't in the picture, but his bio mom Marissa was committed to doing what she needed to do to get David back. Marissa was struggling with drug addiction, however, and it looked like it was going to be a long road of recovery.

Doug and Elissa struggled with anger toward Marissa. They loved David so much, and were furious when they thought about how David was neglected and hurt during his first year of life. They couldn't imagine doing something like that to their own kids, and it was hard for them to empathize and understand where Marissa was coming from. They had weekly visits with Marissa, and it was sometimes tough for Doug and Elissa to treat her kindly, especially if she had a setback with her addiction. And Marissa struggled with them as well. She hated that someone else was taking care of her baby, but addiction is hard to overcome. Marissa had started using drugs with her parents when she was eleven. Doug and Elissa knew the primary goal of foster care was reunification, but if they were honest, sometimes they wondered whether David might be better off staying with them. Sometimes they doubted Marissa would be able to get her act together, and they worried this drawn-out process would end up hurting David more.

Can you relate to Doug and Elissa's story? What about your relationship with your child's birth family have you struggled with the most?

RELATIONSHIPS WITH BIRTH FAMILIES

Most adoptive and foster families will have some level of contact with their child's birth family while raising their child. If you are engaging in foster care, the primary goal is usually reunification, and you will likely have regular (e.g., weekly), supervised visits with the birth family. More and more adoptions are now open rather than closed,[2] meaning there is some contact post-adoption between the adoptive and birth families. This contact can vary in frequency and type according to the preferences of the adoptive and birth families, and can include in-person visits, phone calls, emails or letters, sending pictures, or communication through a third party, among other ways to connect. And even if the adoption is more closed than open, children often attempt to seek out their birth families later in life, which may bring about contact between the adoptive and birth families.

Research has found more benefits than disadvantages to open adoption.[3] Some of the benefits included increased knowledge about oneself and one's history, fewer secrets or unknowns, and having more family in one's life. Interestingly, even when difficulties or challenges arose around contact with one's birth family, adoptees still generally said that openness in adoption was a positive thing in their lives.

In addition to the positive outcomes for your kid, having a relationship with your child's birth family also offers an opportunity to care for a family in need in a unique way. Imagine what might happen if we viewed the journey as not just adopting or fostering a child but adopting or fostering their entire (birth) family. In the adoption and foster community, we talk a lot about caring for children and providing a home for "the least of these." But birth parents who can't care for their children are often also struggling and in need of care and support themselves. It can be difficult for adoptive and foster parents to open their hearts to birth families, and we touch on a few of these reasons in the remainder of this chapter. But caring for your child's birth family can be an amazing example of showing God's love to someone in need.

DEALING WITH YOUR OWN REACTIONS

Before we talk about some ideas for navigating relationships with your child's birth family, it's important we take an honest look at what might come up for us as parents when we engage in this way. If we aren't aware of our own issues and reactions, they are likely to influence our interactions with our child's birth parents, often negatively. Some of the issues that arise for parents and affect their relationships with birth parents include wanting your family to be "normal," wanting to be the child's only parents, wanting to build your family and adopt the child (if they are currently in foster care), having negative views of the birth parents, having safety concerns, and thinking you can care for the child better than the birth parents are able to. These are just a few examples. Think about your life and situation. What feelings or reactions come up for you when you think about your child's birth parents? This is just for your self-awareness, so try not to hold back.

Ideally, you would have a safe relationship where you can process and talk through some of your reactions. For example, if you are married, maybe you can process some of your reactions with your spouse. You might have a small group where you can talk about your feelings and reactions. If it is challenging to find a safe space to talk about your reactions, it might be helpful to think about attending counseling to discuss your reactions. Discuss your feelings with someone else, and don't keep them inside.

Only once you are aware of your feelings and reactions can you make choices about what to do. It's important to recognize what is triggering you and may be influencing your choices. For example, you could say, "I'm feeling really angry toward my child's birth parent because their choices keep hurting my child. I don't want to love them or care for them right now. My natural reaction is to ignore them and be rude to them. But I care about my child and I know that the ultimate goal of foster care is reunification. So I am going to make a conscious choice to be kind to them today even though I don't feel like it."

PRACTICAL SUGGESTIONS FOR RELATIONSHIPS WITH BIRTH FAMILIES

Now that we have taken an honest look at some of our feelings and reactions about having a relationship with our child's birth parents, what are some practical suggestions for navigating this relationship? The type of contact you have with your child's birth family can vary significantly, depending on the directions of the adoption or foster agency, the health of the birth family, and your child's desires and preferences. There isn't one right way to have a relationship with the birth family; lots of different approaches can work.

The best place to begin is to think about how you can include the birth family in the life of your child, to the extent it is safe to do so. For example, it might be possible to have regular in-person meetings or hangouts with the child's birth family. If in-person hangouts are not possible, could you connect via phone or video calls? Could you send photos and letters, updating the birth family about what your child is doing? Could you send them artwork or other crafts your child created? As much as possible, can you include them in the life of your child and family?

BOUNDARIES

Sometimes a birth family might have some serious difficulties or issues, such as struggling with drug use or mental health issues, that make it difficult to connect with them. You might think it is unhealthy for your child to have contact with their birth parents. The relationship with your child's birth parents might make you nervous. If this is your situation, it is always good to check out your feelings with a person you trust or perhaps the adoption or foster agency you are working with. Erin Bouchard, a foster and adoptive parent educator and advocate, notes, "There is a huge difference between unsafe to live with and unsafe to visit."[4] Make sure the limits you are placing on the relationship with the birth parents are in the best interests of the child, and not because of your own discomfort or fear. If it's the latter, it might be good to process your reservations with a counselor.

Still, it can be appropriate to draw boundaries in your relationship with the birth parents. Even in these cases, I suggest thinking about how you can maintain contact in a healthy way. For example, if in-person contact isn't healthy, what about phone or video calls? If phone or video calls aren't healthy, what about letters or sending periodic updates? There is probably a way to maintain some form of contact while maintaining boundaries you are comfortable with. Be creative when making these decisions. For example, if you don't feel comfortable with the birth family knowing your home address, could you set up a PO box to exchange letters? If you don't feel comfortable with the birth family having your cell phone number, could you set up an alternate phone number using a tool like Google Voice, or use video calls to connect?

It's important to explore these options. I counseled a mother whose daughter joined their family through adoption. As the daughter entered her teen years, she desperately wanted to have contact with her birth mother. However, her parents felt that it was not safe to do so, because of her birth mother's previous criminal behavior and mental health issues, and put up a firm "no contact" boundary. This boundary seemed appropriate at the time, but as their daughter got older, she rebelled against it. She started running away and trying to find her birth mother, and when she found her, she ran away to live with her again. This put a huge strain on the parents' relationship with their daughter. I share this example because it was clear their daughter needed to explore her relationship with her birth mother. As parents, you can support your child in that exploration. However, if your child wants to explore that relationship and you don't want to or are unwilling to do so, they will most likely do it without you. Remember, no person or relationship is beyond God's love and ability to redeem. If we truly believe that—and we should—we need to be open to it.

There might be times when you need to take a break from connecting with the birth family. Or your child might want or need to take a break from connecting with their birth family. This is okay; when in doubt, follow the needs and wants of your child. However, keep checking in and trying. Children's attitudes toward their birth family often ebb and flow over time. It's good to keep checking in and do the best you can to help your child connect with their birth family to the extent they want.

Finally, it is important to periodically reevaluate the boundaries you have set with birth parents. In my work with families, I have seen situations where the birth parents make significant healing and progress, but sometimes the adoptive parents still interact with them as though they are unsafe. It's important to check in with yourself. Is the boundary you have set necessary given the current situation?

HELPING YOUR CHILD SEARCH FOR THEIR BIRTH PARENTS

Perhaps your child doesn't know their birth family but would like to find them. As much as possible, it is good to help and assist them in this process. Whether you assist by contacting their adoption or foster agency, helping with research, finding extended family members, or providing emotional support, your child will appreciate that you are in their corner. It can be easy to feel threatened by your child's desire to search for their birth parents, but remember to check in with yourself and your reactions. The birth family will always be a reality in your child's life—this is part of the adoption or foster care process. It doesn't mean your child values you less; rather, this is a normal process of development. If you feel threatened by that exploration, consider processing those feelings with a counselor so it does not hinder your relationship with your child and their birth family.

DOUG AND ELISSA

Check out this dialogue between Doug and Elissa, whom we met in the beginning of this chapter, and their Replanted small group as they discussed some of Elissa's feelings and reactions about connecting with Marissa, the birth mother of their foster son David. (Doug was present but did not speak during this part of the conversation.)

JANNA (GROUP LEADER). Elissa, during the meal you mentioned you were struggling with your feelings about Marissa. Did you want to share more about that?

ELISSA. Yes, I think so. It's kind of hard to share, but I think I need to process it.

JANNA. It's okay, we're all in this together.

ELISSA. Yeah, I know. One of the things I love most about this group is that y'all really get it. So, I feel that lately I've been harboring a lot of resentment and anger toward Marissa in my heart. I know we are called to love and care for her, but it's so hard sometimes. David will be doing so well, and then he goes on a visit with her and comes back, and it's like something has taken over him. He's unhappy, angry, disrespectful . . . And I've seen the way she interacts with him. To put it bluntly, she's mean. I know she came from a hard place, but when she lashes out toward David, it's just so hard to see. We work so hard with him day in and day out, and it breaks my heart that we take steps backward when we have a visit. It's hard not to blame her or think it's all her fault.

GARY (GROUP MEMBER). Elissa, that sounds so hard. Marissa sounds like a real piece of work. I think if I were in your situation, I would feel the same way.

JANNA. Yeah, Elissa, thanks for having the courage to share how you are really feeling. I know that can be uncomfortable—and it's easy to stuff those feelings away.

ELISSA. It's embarrassing, you know? I want to be this great Christian mom and love and serve her. But sometimes I just hate her!

JANNA. And I think that's one of the toughest things about foster care. We have these conflicting emotions—like, you want to love her, but sometimes you hate her. It doesn't always make sense, but both of your emotions are valid and need to be spoken and shared.

ELISSA. Thanks. It does help to say it out loud. I think I've been trying to hide how I feel because I felt that it wasn't right.

What reactions do you have to Elissa's sharing in her small group? Do you have a place where you can be honest and vulnerable about all your feelings, even the difficult ones that you would prefer to hide?

DISCUSSION QUESTIONS

- What stood out to you most as you read this chapter? What did you learn about navigating the relationship with your child's birth family that you didn't know previously?

- What are some key emotions or reactions that come up for you when engaging with your child's birth family? Is there anything you need to talk about or work through so you can be present with your child's birth family?

- What is one thing you would like to try moving forward to improve your relationship with your child's birth family?

18

THRIVING FAMILIES

We have covered a lot of ground together, haven't we? In Part I, we talked about God's heart for families, as well as the importance of being aware of our own issues and expectations. I truly believe God has a huge heart for families and for restoration. I'm guessing you do, too—that might be a big part of the reason you pursued adoption or foster care in the first place. Adoption and foster care are holy work. You are being the hands and feet of Jesus in the most practical way I can imagine—opening your home to a child in need and inviting them to be part of your family.

But it isn't all sunshine and rainbows. Parenting through adoption and foster care can also be very challenging. Many of these challenges are related to the difficult circumstances our children have faced. Many have experienced trauma early in life. Others might not have been able to develop a strong, close relationship with a caregiver, which is the foundation of building a secure attachment. Still others may have serious physical or medical issues that make the daily activities of life a challenge. Adoptive and foster parents have all the regular challenges of parenting alongside these additional challenges. As a trauma-trained therapist, I learned lots of helpful

strategies for assisting kids, but I realized there wasn't an easy
way to share this knowledge with parents. That's one of the
reasons I wrote this book, and one of my goals in continuing
to run the Replanted organization and conference. I want you
to be as prepared as possible for the challenges of parenting.

I'm proud of you for picking up this resource, and I encourage you to continue seeking out more information, training, and
help. No one gives you an instruction manual when you sign
up to be a parent. Even for adoptive and foster parents who
must go through lots of training and home visits and waiting,
there isn't an instruction booklet. You may share many similar
challenges with other parents, but your situation is also unique.

And no book, resource, or therapy will take away the pain
and hurt your child may be dealing with. Healing takes time
and effort, and it doesn't usually happen in a straight line.
When I worked as a therapist, I remember times I spent months
talking, playing, and connecting with a kid—and I went home
after each session feeling that we weren't accomplishing anything. And then one day something would happen—maybe it
was a breakthrough in therapy or something that happened at
school—and the child's direction would make a small shift. All
their problems weren't solved in that instant, but something in
their trajectory had changed. I had a renewed sense of hope
for the future, and a renewed energy for the work.

Keep at it. Even when things seem to not be getting any
better, stay engaged. In my work as a therapist, it often seemed
like the healing process was two steps forward and two steps
backward. Sometimes it was two steps forward and one step
backward, and we would have a small celebration of our
progress. Other times it was one step forward and two steps
backward, and I would get discouraged, wondering whether
all our work was for nothing. If this describes your situation,

stick with it. God doesn't promise us a particular outcome or a particular timeline. We don't know what is around the corner or what the future will bring for ourselves or our children. But God does promise to be with us.

In one of my favorite Bible passages, Jesus says, "I have told you these things, so that in me you may have peace. In this world you will have trouble. But take heart! I have overcome the world" (John 16:33). We will have trouble in this world. Our kids will have trouble, and our families will have trouble. There isn't a way to get around that reality. But we can have peace, and we don't lose heart, because Jesus is with us.

In addition to having Jesus with us, we also need a community of people around us. We can't do the adoption or foster care parenting journey alone. It's too difficult and too unique of an experience. We need people around us who understand our situation and can give us grace. We need someone who can give us a hug or bring us a casserole when we need it. That's the reason I started Replanted, so adoptive and foster families (both parents and kids) could be in community with each other and know they aren't alone. If you don't have a community of people around you who are supporting you in your journey, reach out to Replanted, join us on social media, or come to our conference. We need each other. We weren't meant to do life alone.

Also, it's critical for us to listen to the voices in the adoption and foster community who have been marginalized for so long. They have a lot to teach us about how to engage effectively with our children. We need to be open to these perspectives, even if they are challenging and different from our own perspective. Some foster and adoptee voices that I recommend learning from are Cam Lee Small (@TherapyRedeemed), Angela Tucker (@AngieAdoptee), and Tori Hope Petersen (@

ToriHopePetersen), among others. We need to listen to adult adoptees, former foster youth, and birth parents.

Keep digging in and doing your own work. We never "arrive" as a parent. Just as our child's healing is a process, so our growth and development as a parent is a process. Never stop growing and learning. Never stop working on your issues and hang-ups. If you have a strong reaction to something, it's a good clue that something is being triggered inside you. Don't be afraid to get more help and go to counseling. It's difficult to take our child to a place of healing we haven't been to ourselves.

Know that I am praying for you and rooting for you. I'm so proud of the work you are doing day in and day out for your kids. God sees all your effort, too, and God is proud of you and loves you. God sees the prayers, tears, meals, difficult conversations, doctor's appointments, and school meetings. You are doing God's work faithfully through the many ups and downs that come with adoptive and foster parenting. God loves your kids more than you could ever imagine, God loves their birth parents more than you could ever imagine, and God loves you more than you could ever imagine. Don't ever forget you are God's beloved, and you are not alone. And if you come to the Replanted Conference, make sure you stop me and say hello!

DISCUSSION QUESTIONS

- What are two or three of the main takeaways that came up for you as you read this final chapter?
- How do you think God sees you in your parenting journey? What do you feel God saying to you right now?
- What would it look like to get more involved in a community of other families who understand your situation? What is one step you could take toward getting more connected?

Appendix

HELPFUL RESOURCES

BOOKS

Berry, Mike. *Confessions of an Adoptive Parent: Hope and Help from the Trenches of Foster Care and Adoption.* Eugene, OR: Harvest House, 2018.

Gray, Deborah D. *Attaching through Love, Hugs, and Play: Simple Strategies to Help Build Connections with Your Child.* London: Jessica Kingsley, 2014.

Hoffman, Kent, Glen Cooper, and Bert Powell. *Raising a Secure Child: How Circle of Security Parenting Can Help You Nurture Your Child's Attachment, Emotional Resilience, and Freedom to Explore.* New York: Guilford Press, 2017.

Hook, Jenn Ranter, Joshua N. Hook, and Mike R. Berry. *Replanted: Faith-Based Support for Adoptive and Foster Families.* West Conshohocken, PA: Templeton Press, 2019.

Johnson, Jason. *Everyone Can Do Something: A Field Guide for Strategically Rallying Your Church around the Orphaned and Vulnerable.* Grand Rapids: Credo House, 2018.

———. *Reframing Foster Care: Filtering Your Foster Parenting Journey through the Lens of the Gospel.* Grand Rapids: Credo House, 2018.

Kranowitz, Carol Stock. *The Out-of-Sync Child: Recognizing and Coping with Sensory Processing Disorder*. New York: Skylight Press, 2006.

Purvis, Karyn B., David R. Cross, and Wendy Lyons Sunshine. *The Connected Child: Bring Hope and Healing to Your Adoptive Family*. New York: McGraw-Hill, 2007.

Purvis, Karyn, Lisa Qualls. *The Connected Parent: Real-Life Strategies for Building Trust and Attachment*. Eugene, OR: Harvest House, 2020

Siegel, Daniel J., and Tina Payne Bryson. *No-Drama Discipline: The Whole-Brain Way to Calm the Chaos and Nurture Your Child's Developing Mind*. New York: Bantam Books, 2016.

———. *The Whole-Brain Child: 12 Revolutionary Strategies to Nurture Your Child's Developing Mind*. New York: Bantam Books, 2012.

ORGANIZATIONS
Replanted (ReplantedMinistry.org)

Honestly Adoption (HonestlyAdoption.com)

Tapestry (TapestryMinistry.org)

The Adoption Connection (TheAdoptionConnection.com)

CONFERENCES
Christian Alliance for Orphans (CAFO) Summit (CAFO.org)

Replanted Conference (ReplantedConference.org)

Re: Conference (RealEncouragement.org)

TRAININGS
Trust-Based Relational Intervention (TBRI) (Child.TCU.edu)

Empowered to Connect (EmpoweredtoConnect.org)

ACKNOWLEDGEMENTS

Writing a book is definitely a collective effort, and there are so many people who have supported me throughout this process. First, to my husband, Josh, you have been my biggest cheerleader and helped bring this book to fruition. Thanks for sharing in my passion to see foster and adoptive families supported, especially the kids. Your unwavering support, encouragement, and love has meant the world to me.

To Autumn, you made me a mom. You have taught me some of life's greatest lessons and I'm grateful every day that I get to do life with you.

To Herald Press, thank you so much for believing in this book and sharing our desire to provide much needed support to foster and adoptive families. You have been incredible to work with and have made this book so much better than we could have imagined.

To all the children who shared their stories with me while I worked as a trauma therapist in foster care. This book reflects your stories, feelings, and experiences. You opened my eyes to the realities of your experiences—that with adoption and foster care, there is often beauty but also loss. Thank you for allowing me to walk alongside you in all the joys, losses, and questions you experienced. May this journey for others never be the same because of the wisdom you imparted.

Lastly, I want to thank my Replanted team—from the countless leaders around the country creating safe spaces for families to be supported, to my conference planning team breathing life and vision into an experience that transforms lives. It's been a privilege linking arms with you.

—Jenn Ranter Hook

NOTES

CHAPTER 2

1. C. Csaky, *Keeping Children Out of Harmful Institutions: Why We Should Be Investing in Family-Based Care* (London: Save the Children, 2009).

2. National Center for Missing and Exploited Children, "Our Impact," accessed July 29, 2022 https://www.missingkids.org/content/ncmec/en/ourwork/impact.html.

CHAPTER 3

1. M. Steele, J. Hodges, J. Kaniuk, S. Hillman, and K. Henderson, "Attachment Representations and Adoption: Associations between Maternal States of Mind and Emotion Narratives in Previously Maltreated Children," *Journal of Child Psychotherapy* 29, no. 2 (2003): 187–205; H. Steele, M. Steele, and P. Fonagy, "Associations among Attachment Classifications of Mothers, Fathers, and Their Infants," *Child Development* 67 (1996): 541–55.

2. See K. Hoffman, G. Cooper, and B. Powell, *Raising a Secure Child: How Circle of Security Parenting Can Help You Nurture Your Child's Attachment, Emotional Resilience, and Freedom to Explore* (New York: Guilford Press, 2017).

CHAPTER 4

1. F. Swan (@fereraswan), Instagram [photo], January 18, 2022, https://www.instagram.com/p/CY316ZDObav/.

2. C. Csaky, *Keeping Children Out of Harmful Institutions: Why We Should Be Investing in Family-Based Care* (London: Save the Children, 2009).

3. M. R. Hammer, M. J. Bennett, and R. Wiseman, "Measuring Intercultural Sensitivity: The Intercultural Development Inventory," *International Journal of Intercultural Relations* 27 (2003): 421–33.

CHAPTER 5

1. J. Bromberg, "Trauma, Identity, and Love: Being Adopted Didn't Give Me a Better Life, but Changed My Path," *USA Today*, November 27, 2021, https://www.usatoday.com/story/opinion/2021/11/27/adopted-children-live-trauma-rejection-but-education-can-help/8736589002/.

2. Child Welfare Information Gateway, *Parenting a Child Who Has Experienced Trauma* (Washington, DC: US Department of Health and Human Services, Children's Bureau, 2014).

3. P. Walker, *Complex PTSD: From Surviving to Thriving* (Lafayette, CA: Azure Coyote, 2013).

4. The following points are drawn from Child Welfare Information Gateway, *Parenting a Child*.

5. J. D. Bremmer, "Traumatic Stress: Effects on the Brain," *Dialogues in Clinical Neuroscience* 8, no. 4 (2006): 445–61.

6. I. Smith, "How Does Trauma Affect the Brain? And What It Means for You," Whole Wellness Therapy, June 29, 2020, https://www.wholewellness therapy.com/post/trauma-and-the-brain.

7. These key factors are drawn from Child Welfare Information Gateway, *Parenting a Child*.

8. Centers for Disease Control and Prevention, "Risk and Protective Factors," last reviewed January 5, 2021, https://www.cdc.gov/violenceprevention/aces/riskprotectivefactors.html.

9. J. A. Cohen et al., "Practice Parameter for the Assessment and Treatment of Children and Adolescents with Posttraumatic Stress Disorder," *Journal of the American Academy of Child and Adolescent Psychiatry* 49, no. 4 (2010): 414–30.

10. L. van Dernoot Lipsky with C. Burk, *Trauma Stewardship: An Everyday Guide to Caring for Self While Caring for Others* (San Francisco: Berrett-Koehler, 2009)

11. J. R. Hook, J. N. Hook, and M. Berry, *Replanted: Faith-Based Support for Adoptive and Foster Families* (West Conshohocken, PA: Templeton Press, 2019).

CHAPTER 6

1. H. F. Harlow, "The Nature of Love," *American Psychologist* 13, no. 12 (1958): 673–85.

2. J. Bowlby, "Forty-Four Juvenile Thieves: Their Characters and Home Lives," *International Journal of Psychoanalysis* 25 (1944): 19–52.

3. J. Bowlby, *Attachment*, vol. 1 in *Attachment and Loss* (New York: Basic Books, 1969).

4. M. D. Ainsworth and S. M. Bell, "Attachment, Exploration, and Separation: Illustrated by the Behavior of One-Year-Olds in a Strange Situation," *Child Development* 41, no. 1 (1970): 49–67.

5. M. Main and J. Solomon, "Discovery of a New, Insecure-Disorganized/Disoriented Attachment Pattern," in *Affective Development in Infancy*, ed. M. Yogman and T. B. Brazelton (Norwood, NJ: Ablex, 1986), 95–124.

6. M. G. Quiroga and C. Hamilton-Giachritsis, "Attachment Styles in Children Living in Alternative Care: A Systematic Review of the Literature," *Child Youth Care Forum* 45 (2016): 625–53.

7. American Psychiatric Association, *Diagnostic and Statistical Manual of Mental Disorders*, 5th ed. (Arlington, VA: American Psychiatric Association, 2013).

CHAPTER 7

1. T. Hendler et al., "Sensing the Invisible: Differential Sensitivity of Visual Cortex and Amygdala to Traumatic Context," *NeuroImage* 19, no. 3 (2003): 587–600; G. Serafini et al., "The Relationship between Sensory Processing Patterns, Alexithymia, Traumatic Childhood Experiences, and Quality of Life among Patients with Unipolar and Bipolar Disorders," *Child Abuse and Neglect* 62 (2016): 39–59.

2. J. R. Hook, J. N. Hook, and M. Berry, *Replanted: Faith-Based Support for Adoptive and Foster Families* (West Conshohocken, PA: Templeton Press, 2019).

3. C. S. Kranowitz, *The Out-of-Sync Child: Recognizing and Coping with Sensory Processing Disorder* (New York: Skylight Press, 2006).

4. There is some debate in the field about whether sensory processing difficulties constitute unique disorders or are symptoms of other disorders. For example, sensory processing disorders do not appear in the most recent edition of the *Diagnostic and Statistical Manual of Mental Disorders* (*DSM-5*), which is the primary resource for mental health disorders. For me, the debate is interesting but perhaps not practically important. Some children will struggle with sensory processing difficulties, and the key question is, What can we do to help them?

5. Kranowitz, *Out-of-Sync Child*.

6. Kranowitz.

7. Kranowitz.

CHAPTER 8

1. The Implicit Association Test is available from the nonprofit Project Implicit at https://implicit.harvard.edu/implicit/takeatest.html.

2. J. N. Hook, D. E. Davis, J. Owen, and C. DeBlaere, *Cultural Humility: Engaging Diverse Identities in Therapy* (Washington, DC: APA Books, 2017).

3. N. Weaver, "The History of Transracial Adoption," Adoption Network Cleveland: The Ohio Family Connection, October 18, 2018, https://www.adoptionnetwork.org/news-events/archive.html/article/2018/10/18/the-history-of-transracial-adoption.

CHAPTER 9

1. E. Kübler-Ross, *On Death and Dying: What the Dying Have to Teach Doctors, Nurses, Clergy and Their Own Families* (New York: Macmillan, 1969).

2. H. G. Prigerson and P. K. Maciejewski, "Grief and Acceptance as Opposite Sides of the Same Coin: Setting a Research Agenda to Study Peaceful Acceptance of Loss," *British Journal of Psychiatry* 193, no. 6 (December 2008): 435–37, https://doi.org/10.1192/bjp.bp.108.053157.

CHAPTER 10

1. R. M. Krieder and P. N. Cohen, "Disability among Internationally Adopted Children in the United States," *Pediatrics* 124, no. 5 (2009): 1311–318.

2. The following questions are from Jennifer L. Lile, "Adopting a Child with Special Needs," Special Needs Alliance, January 11, 2021, https://www.specialneedsalliance.org/blog/adopting-a-child-with-special-needs/.

3. The following points draw from R. McClure, "How to Advocate for Students in Special Education," Very Well Family, last modified June 6, 2022, https://www.verywellfamily.com/how-to-advocate-for-students-with-special-needs-617206.

4. For more information on the Individuals with Disabilities Education Act, see https://sites.ed.gov/idea/.

CHAPTER 11

1. A. H. Maslow, *Motivation and Personality* (New York: Harper and Row, 1954).

2. B. A. van der Kolk, *The Body Keeps the Score: Brain, Mind, and Body in the Healing of Trauma* (New York: Penguin Books, 2014).

3. See K. B. Purvis, D. R. Cross, D. R. Dansereau, and S. R. Parris, "Trust-Based Relational Intervention (TBRI): A Systemic Approach to Complex Developmental Trauma," *Child and Youth Services* 34, no. 4 (2013): 360–86.

4. K. B. Purvis, D. R. Cross, D. R. Dansereau, and S. R. Parris, "Trust-Based Relational Intervention (TBRI): A Systemic Approach to Complex

Developmental Trauma," *Child and Youth Services* 34, no. 4 (2013): 360–86.

5. R. Beauvais, "Healing PTSD through Relationships and Touch," Behavioral Health News, January 1, 2013, https://www.behavioralhealthnews.org/healing-ptsd-through-relationship-and-touch/.

6. A. M. Jernberg and P. B. Booth, *Theraplay: Helping Parents and Children Build Better Relationships through Attachment-Based Play*, 2nd ed. (San Francisco: Jossey-Bass, 1999).

7. Karyn Purvis Institute of Child Development, "Gift 6: Give Your Child Playfulness," YouTube video, May 29, 2015, 1:32, https://www.youtube.com/watch?v=bH2No-G9LXc.

CHAPTER 12

1. S. Brown, *Play: How It Shapes the Brain, Opens the Imagination, and Invigorates the Soul* (New York: Avery Trade, 2009).

2. J. Panksepp, "The Riddle of Laughter: Neural and Psychoevolutionary Underpinnings of Joy," *Current Directions in Psychological Science* 9 (2000): 183–86.

3. K. B. Purvis, D. R. Cross, and W. L. Sunshine, *The Connected Child: Bringing Hope and Healing to Your Adoptive Family* (New York: McGraw-Hill, 2007).

CHAPTER 13

1. See B. A. van der Kolk, *The Body Keeps the Score: Brain, Mind, and Body in the Healing of Trauma* (New York: Penguin Books, 2014).

2. K. B. Purvis, D. R. Cross, and W. L. Sunshine, *The Connected Child: Bringing Hope and Healing to Your Adoptive Family* (New York: McGraw-Hill, 2007).

3. D. J. Siegel and T. P. Bryson, *No-Drama Discipline: The Whole-Brain Way to Calm the Chaos and Nurture Your Child's Developing Mind* (New York: Bantam Books, 2016).

4. R. Greene, *The Explosive Child: A New Approach for Understanding and Parenting Easily Frustrated, Chronically Inflexible Children* (New York: Harper, 2021).

5. A. Heilmann et al., "Physical Punishment and Child Outcomes: A Narrative Review of Prospective Studies," *The Lancet* 398, no. 10297 (2021): 355–64.

6. Quoted in B. L. Smith, "The Case against Spanking," *APA Monitor* 43, no. 4 (2012): 60.

CHAPTER 14

1. See S. Pelini, "An Age-by-Age Guide to Helping Kids Manage Emotions," Gottman Institute, last modified February 3, 2021, https://www.gottman .com/blog/age-age-guide-helping-kids-manage-emotions/.
2. Pelini.
3. S. E. Trehub, N. Ghazban, and M. Corbeil, "Musical Affect Regulation in Infancy," *Annals of the New York Academy of Science* 1337 (2015): 186–92.
4. M. K. Rothbart, H. Ziaie, and C. G. O'Boyle, "Self-Regulation and Emotion in Infancy," *New Directions for Child and Adolescent Development* 55 (1992): 7–23.
5. Pelini.
6. S. Pelini, "Teaching Your Child to Manage Anger and Anxiety," Raising Independent Kids, April 30, 2017, https://raising-independent-kids.com/ 1163-2/.
7. F. R. Morris and D. G. Morris, *The Recognition and Expression of Feelings* (South Bend, IN: TACM, 1985).
8. These ideas are drawn from Pelini, "Manage Anger and Anxiety."

CHAPTER 15

1. P. Goodyear-Brown, *Play Therapy with Traumatized Children: A Prescriptive Approach* (Hoboken, NJ: Wiley, 2010).
2. G. Egan, *The Skilled Helper*, 3rd ed. (Belmont, CA: Brooks/Cole, 1986), 100–102.

CHAPTER 17

1. J. Finn (@FostertheFamilyBlog), "I talked with a birth mother friend of mine today. She was an addict who destroyed her life and her family's lives, and now she's a living, breathing example of a life radically transformed," Facebook, July 14, 2019, https://www.facebook.com/fosterthefamilyblog/ photos/a.1576775475984841/2298756803786701/.
2. D. H. Siegel, "Growing Up in Open Adoption: Young Adults' Perspectives," *Families in Society: The Journal of Contemporary Social Services* 93, no. 2 (2012): 133–40.
3. Siegel.
4. E. Bouchard (@traumainformedparenting), Instagram [photo], August 8, 2022, https://www.instagram.com/p/ChAza_YOw3T/?igshid=YmMyMTA 2M2Y%3D.

THE AUTHORS

Jenn Ranter Hook is the founder and executive director of Replanted. She previously worked as a trauma therapist for children and adolescents in foster care. She speaks frequently on topics related to adoption and foster care support, mental health, and trauma. She is also the author of *Replanted: Faith-Based Support for Foster and Adoptive Families*, and lives in Dallas, Texas, with her husband Josh and daughter Autumn.

Joshua N. Hook, PhD, is a professor of counseling psychology at the University of North Texas and is a licensed clinical psychologist (LCP). He has written or cowritten six other books, including *Replanted: Faith-Based Support for Foster and Adoptive Families*. He blogs regularly about psychology and faith at JoshuaNHook.com. He lives in Dallas, Texas, with his wife Jenn and daughter Autumn.